Table of Contents

Practice Test #1..4
  Practice Questions..4
    Language and Literacy...4
    Mathematics...9
    Social Studies...13
    Science..16
    Health and Physical Education...18
    Creative and Performing Arts..20
  Answers and Explanations..22
    Language and Literacy...22
    Mathematics...28
    Social Studies...34
    Science..38
    Health and Physical Education...41
    Creative and Performing Arts..44
Practice Test #2..46
  Practice Questions..46
    Language and Literacy...46
    Mathematics...51
    Social Studies...56
    Science..58
    Health and Physical Education...61
    Creative and Performing Arts..62
  Answers and Explanations..65
    Language and Literacy...65
    Mathematics...70
    Social Studies...75
    Science..79
    Health and Physical Education...81
    Creative and Performing Arts..83

Practice Test #1

Practice Questions

Language and Literacy

1. One of the easiest tasks for phonological awareness is:
    a. Replacing sounds to make new words
    b. Hearing rhyming sounds within words
    c. Isolating and classifying words sounds
    d. Blending and/or separation of sounds

2. Which of the following phonological awareness activities is easiest for children?
    a. Naming rhyming words for a word
    b. Picking rhyming words from lists
    c. Recognizing words that rhyme
    d. These are all equally difficult.

3. Of the following, which is a correct definition of the term phonics?
    a. Knowing all alphabet letters
    b. Sound to letter relationships
    c. Recognizing sounds in words
    d. Manipulating speech sounds

4. Being read to in early childhood helps develop metalinguistic abilities. Young children can tell stories in books through the pictures; eventually they understand that the words printed in the books are connected to spoken words. This is an example of which of these four metalinguistic abilities?
    a. Word consciousness
    b. Conventions of print
    c. The functions of print
    d. Reading with fluency

5. The sentence "They am going out to dinner" is incorrect:
    a. Syntactically.
    b. Semantically.
    c. Grammatically.
    d. Morphologically.

6. Which component of oral language development involves the social rules for using language?
    a. The pragmatic component
    b. The phonological component
    c. The semantic component
    d. The syntactic component

7. When very young children begin to produce idiomorphs, this is part of which stage of oral language development?
    a. The Cooing stage
    b. The One-Word stage
    c. The Telegraphic stage
    d. The Babbling stage

8. For children learning English as a second language (ESL), which stage of second-language acquisition is the earliest wherein they can understand jokes told in English all or most of the time?
    a. Early Production
    b. Speech Emergence
    c. Intermediate Fluency
    d. Advanced Fluency

9. If a child who is 9–10 years old does not correctly pronounce the phonemes /s/ and /r/, what does this most likely represent?
    a. A definite sign of hearing loss
    b. A kind of intellectual disability
    c. Normal language development
    d. A possible articulation disorder

10. Which of the following is a cause for concern that a young child's speech and language development may be delayed?
    a. An 18-month-old points and waves but does not speak to communicate.
    b. An 18-month-old uses gestures more often than voice to communicate.
    c. An 18-month-old imitates adult speech sounds but does not say words.
    d. An 18-month-old can speak, but parents cannot understand most of it.

11. In learning the alphabetic principle, which do children typically develop first?
    a. They learn the shapes of letters.
    b. They learn the sounds of letters.
    c. They learn these all concurrently.
    d. They learn the names of letters.

12. Which of the following is a consideration for students learning English as a second language (ESL) when their native language is Spanish?
    a. There are more vowel sounds in Spanish than English.
    b. English is taught in syllables, but Spanish in phonemes.
    c. Spanish initial consonant clusters are absent in English.
    d. Pronunciation of letters in English is more complicated.

13. What statement accurately reflects the findings of research into print awareness in preschoolers?
    a. Four-year-olds have commonly mastered both print and word concepts.
    b. Four-year-olds' print awareness skills do not predict future reading skills.
    c. Four-year-olds may learn many word concepts earlier than print concepts.
    d. Four-year-olds may learn many print concepts earlier than word concepts.

14. Of the following, which lists typical stages of learning to read in the correct chronological order?
    a. Orthographic reading; alphabetic reading; reading by phonetic cues; reading logographically
    b. Reading by phonetic cues; orthographic reading; reading logographically; alphabetic reading
    c. Reading logographically; reading by phonetic cues; alphabetic reading; orthographic reading
    d. Alphabetic reading; orthographic reading; reading logographically; reading by phonetic cues

15. Which statement is most accurate regarding children who have good reading comprehension?
    a. They read material which is familiar within their existing knowledge.
    b. They are skilled at decoding, so they do not need good vocabularies.
    c. They can summarize what they read and predict what will come next.
    d. They comprehend text without needing to use the sentence structure.

16. A beginning reader unfamiliar with seeing the homophones "reads" and "reeds" in print deduces the meaning of plants, not perusal, from the sentence "Reeds grow in marshes" because the former makes sense in the sentence while the latter does not. This is an example of using _____ to aid comprehension.
    a. Phonics
    b. Context
    c. Spelling
    d. Pictures

17. In children's literature, what do picture books represent?
    a. These represent a genre.
    b. Both a genre and a format
    c. These represent a format
    d. Neither genre nor format.

18. Which of the following characteristics in children's books is NOT helpful to early literacy development?
    a. All are
    b. Pictures
    c. Rhyming
    d. Repetition

19. When they choose children's literature, what should adults seek?
    a. Moralistic themes
    b. Use of stereotypes
    c. Unbelievable fantasies
    d. Knowledgeable authors

20. Regarding indicators that a child may have dyslexia, which statement is generally most accurate?
    a. The child always sounds out words but takes much longer.
    b. The child finds reading sentences harder than single words.
    c. The child scores consistently with ability on objective tests.
    d. The child has equal difficulty reading short and long words.

21. Which of these is true about children's development of spelling?
    a. Children must be able to read words to spell them.
    b. Children can spell without knowing letter patterns.
    c. Children usually can read words that they can spell.
    d. Children do not infer spelling of new spoken words.

22. During which stage of spelling development do children typically first start to understand correspondences of alphabet letters to speech sounds?
    a. In the Transitional stage
    b. During the Correct stage
    c. During the Phonetic stage
    d. In the Semiphonetic stage

23. Research with preschoolers has found which of the following about invented spellings?
    a. Individual preschoolers each invent their own unique spellings.
    b. Most of various preschoolers' invented spellings are the same.
    c. The spellings that preschoolers invent are influenced by adults.
    d. When preschoolers' invented spellings match, this is by chance.

24. What can be said with the most certainty about a child who, when asked to say the first sound in the word "cow," responds by saying "Moo"?
    a. The child must have some kind of hearing loss.
    b. The child must not have phonemic awareness.
    c. The child must not know the alphabet's letters.
    d. The child must have some intellectual disability.

25. In which stage of children's writing development do they first realize that meanings are expressed by written symbols?
    a. Scribbling and drawing stage
    b. The stage with writing letters
    c. The letters and spaces stage
    d. Letter-like forms and shapes

26. Which of the following is true about children's writing skills?
    a. Writing skills and reading skills reciprocally improve one another.
    b. Writing skills are not apt to enhance learning as reading skills are.
    c. Writing skills come naturally to children and need not be taught.
    d. Writing skills meet any purpose or audience with the same style.

27. In the POWER strategy, which of the five writing steps in this model is one that students are notorious for most often neglecting?
    a. Organization
    b. Rewriting
    c. Planning
    d. Editing

28. One scale for assessing children's emerging writing skills rates three areas of composition. Of these, which one includes identifying whether the child understands the concept of symbolic representation?
    a. The Language Level
    b. Directional Principles
    c. The Message Quality
    d. None of these does.

29. In the past, a traditional practice of many teachers was to judge student compositions by:
    a. Function more than form.
    b. Form and function equally.
    c. Neither form nor function.
    d. Form more than function.

30. For someone to read a student's composition, which of the following writing conventions will be the *first* to interfere with perceiving the writer's message if it is of poor quality and contains many errors?
    a. Capitalization
    b. Construction
    c. Punctuation
    d. Handwriting

31. Of the following, which sentence is correctly punctuated?
    a. "I told you that it would be ready next week; it will be ready next week."
    b. "I told you, that it would be ready next week it will be ready next week."
    c. "I told you that it would be ready next week, it will be ready next week."
    d. "I told you that it would be ready next week it will be ready next week."

32. Which of these words is misspelled?
    a. Simulacrum
    b. Stimulate
    c. Simularly
    d. Simulate

33. Which of the following sentences uses correct capitalization?
    a. "This bill was signed into law by the President."
    b. "Some of our cousins lived in Washington, D.C."
    c. "He wrote that he plans to come South to visit."
    d. "My classes include English, Science, and Math."

34. What has research shown about children's invented spellings in writing relative to their spelling and reading development?
    a. Invented spelling improves reading, but shortens writings.
    b. Invented spelling impedes word analysis skill development.
    c. Invented spelling interferes with children's correct spelling.
    d. Invented spelling enhances both spelling and reading skills.

35. Which statement is true about how teachers can help motivate young children to write?
   a. Enthusiasm is sustained by diverse writing activities and examples of a variety of writing.
   b. Providing children "fun" writing activities will prevent them from taking writing seriously.
   c. Making deliberate transcribing errors as children dictate will only give them wrong ideas.
   d. Young children should take turns writing an entire class newsletter rather than only parts.

36. Which of these have writing teachers found about student motivation to write?
   a. Students work harder on writing assignments only their teacher will see.
   b. Students expend more effort on writing that will be posted in classrooms.
   c. Students are inhibited from doing their best if classmates will be hearing it.
   d. Students who are home-schooled have no chance to write for an audience.

Mathematics

37. Of the following, which is accurate regarding the relationship of problem-solving skills to math?
   a. Children are not interested in solving everyday problems; adults must give incentives.
   b. Children learn mathematical thinking; other things promote language and social skills.
   c. Children learn through solving problems that there can be multiple possible solutions.
   d. Children should not propose problems or ask questions about them; the adults should.

38. When children develop good problem-solving skills, how does this affect related characteristics?
   a. Problem-solving skills promote abilities with self-regulation.
   b. Problem-solving skills promote rigidity more than flexibility.
   c. Problem-solving skills promote impatience over persistence.
   d. Problem-solving skills promote the dangerous taking of risks.

39. Which of these adult behaviors is most conducive to developing children's reasoning skills?
   a. When adults analyze children's thought processes and then explain them to the children
   b. When adults ask children questions, allow them time to think, and listen to their answers
   c. When adults tell children why something exists/is a certain way and discuss it with them
   d. When adults classify objects or concepts into groups to demonstrate logic to the children

40. To help young children reason logically about math and science concepts, what should adults use?
   a. Only abstract examples to stimulate higher order cognitive skills
   b. Concrete objects like toys, crayons and paper, and their fingers
   c. Pictures, diagrams, and charts they draw that illustrate concepts
   d. (B) and (C) are both better for young children than (A) would be

41. What is true about how adults and children communicate about mathematics?
   a. It helps children clarify their thoughts to converse with adults, but not to converse with peers.
   b. Communicating about math problems furthers mathematical thinking, but not any other skills.
   c. Diagrams and symbols help children understand math concepts, but words and pictures do not.
   d. Reading children's books together that combine numbers, rhymes, and repetition is efficacious.

42. Expert advice on games and activities adults can use to develop children's early math skills is best represented by which of the following?

    a. Adults should ask children guiding questions as in the Socratic Method rather than giving answers.

    b. Adults should propose math story problems to young children according to their age/grade levels.

    c. Adults should not pose problems like division to toddlers as they lack the capacity to handle them.

    d. Adults should use unfamiliar objects in story problems because familiar ones will distract children.

43. Of the following, which most helps young children connect mathematics to real life?

    a. Formal math instruction in school

    b. Describing activities in math words

    c. Using novel manipulatives in math

    d. Original examples of new concepts

44. When adults play with young children at pouring liquid into differently sized and shaped containers, which mathematical skill(s) does this develop?

    a. All these and more

    b. Measurement

    c. Conservation

    d. Estimation

45. Which of the following is true about representation skills relative to young children?

    a. Children will not develop representation skills until they are older.

    b. Children are not using representation when they count on fingers.

    c. Children draw pictures because they have no representation skills.

    d. Children show representation in make-believe play and tally marks.

46. How can a teacher help a young child apply math process skills during typical preschool activities?

    a. When a child sorts toys by color, the teacher describes this as classification.

    b. When a child sorts toys by color, the teacher asks how s/he is sorting them.

    c. When a child sorts toys by color, the teacher asks how else s/he might sort.

    d. When a child sorts toys by color, these all apply varying math process skills.

47. Which of the following is true regarding children's development of number sense?

    a. Children must learn all number names before they learn to count.

    b. Children learn to count before learning all the names of numbers.

    c. Children's number sense is equal to, and a synonym for, counting.

    d. Children's number sense is that numbers only describe quantities.

48. What can adults do to help young children develop their number sense and numeracy skills?

    a. Counting real objects in the environment is very useful.

    b. Sorting by color, shape, or size is irrelevant to numbers.

    c. Sorting by difference is better than sorting by similarity.

    d. Sorting by similarity is better than sorting by difference.

49. Which of the following are considered operations in mathematics?
    a. Adding and squaring
    b. Numbers and fractions
    c. Quotients and remainders
    d. Minuends and subtrahends

50. In the mathematical order of operations, which of these is true?
    a. Exponents are done before adding, subtracting, multiplying, or dividing.
    b. Calculations outside parentheses are done before those inside of them.
    c. Addition and subtraction are done before multiplication and division are.
    d. Multiplication is done before division and addition is before subtraction.

51. What is correct regarding patterns and relationships relative to early math development?
    a. Awareness and understanding of them let children understand categorization and rhythm.
    b. Awareness and understanding of them let children know structure, but not predict events.
    c. Awareness and understanding of them let children learn algebra, but do not aid geometry.
    d. Awareness and understanding of them let children do math, but do not aid art or music.

52. How can adults prepare young children for content mathematics via patterns and relationships?
    a. They can help them identify patterns in fabric prints, but not art.
    b. Helping them string beads in alternating colors teaches patterns.
    c. Dance steps are too complex for young children to comprehend.
    d. Regularly alternating two colors 1:1 is the most that they can do.

53. Of three essential concepts in all mathematics models, which is naturally most familiar to children?
    a. Change
    b. Part-Whole
    c. Comparison
    d. None of these

54. To help young children understand the concept of change in mathematics, in which instructional sequence is it best for teachers to have them progress?
    a. First abstract, then concrete, then pictorial
    b. First pictorial, then abstract, then concrete
    c. First concrete, then pictorial, then abstract
    d. These should be combined simultaneously.

55. To help young children learn about geometric shapes, figures, and angles, adults can first tell them the names of these while they look at them together. Thereafter, in which sequence should adults do the following exercises with young children?
    a. Have them name shapes; describe them; trace drawings of them; finger-draw them in air; draw them
    b. Have them describe shapes; name them; trace drawings of them; draw them; finger-draw them in air
    c. Have them trace drawings of shapes; finger-draw them in air; draw them; describe them; name them
    d. Have them draw shapes; trace drawings of them; finger-draw them in air; name them; describe them

56. What things can adults best use to help very young children learn geometric concepts?
    a. Concrete objects
    b. Both of these
    c. Everyday activities
    d. Neither of these

57. Of the following, which is the most relevant definition of measurement relative to young children's learning early math skills?
    a. It enables children to see relationships among things in the real world, during everyday life.
    b. It is the process of determining the lengths, widths, heights, and weights of physical objects.
    c. It is a formal way to count time in seconds, minutes, hours, days, weeks, months, years, etc.
    d. It is a method whereby children can understand sizes of things, but not compare their sizes.

58. What is most appropriate for young children to learn and practice measurement as an early mathematical skill?
    a. Adults should discourage children's choosing measuring units and teach standard ones immediately.
    b. Letting young children choose their own measurement units (like toys) promotes early development.
    c. When children help with everyday activities, discussing measurement will make participation less fun.
    d. Adults can let children express measurements using toys, etc., but should not also do this themselves.

59. Which of these is true about what young children typically understand about time measurement and how adults can help them learn about it?
    a. Asking simple questions about relative durations promotes comparison skills.
    b. Adults should not talk about minutes until children understand their meaning.
    c. Telling young children how long everyday activities took teaches them nothing.
    d. Even the youngest children understand terms like yesterday, today, and tomorrow.

60. According to Piaget's theory of cognitive development, how do very young children approach the ideas of part-whole and fractions?
    a. They typically think several pieces of an apple equal more fruit than one whole apple.
    b. They typically understand that pieces are parts of a whole even at the youngest ages.
    c. They typically recognize fractions as parts of a whole if they can use concrete objects.
    d. They typically see wholes as more than parts, but not how many parts make a whole.

61. To help young children practice the collection, organization, and display of data, which of the following activities would be most relevant?
    a. A teacher lets children choose differently shaped stickers and identify what those shapes are
    b. A teacher lets children choose differently colored stickers and guess numbers of colors picked
    c. A teacher lets children choose differently colored stickers and match them to colors on a chart
    d. A teacher lets children choose differently colored stickers as cumulative rewards toward prizes

62. National standards for mathematics instruction dictate that children from preschool through second grade should be able to do which of these relative to data-based inferences and predictions?
    a. Be able to talk about events as "likely" or "unlikely" based on their experiences
    b. Be able to propose predictions and justify them based on data that they gather
    c. Be able to collect and analyze data, draw conclusions, and justify them with data
    d. Be able to make inferences/predictions and design studies to investigate these

63. One simple model to teach inference to young children makes certain assumptions. Which of the following accurately reflects one of these assumptions?
    a. Inferring eliminates the need to seek clues to get answers.
    b. We must use newly found clues, not what we already know.
    c. When we infer something, we have to be able to support it.
    d. To infer, we must first know there is only one right answer.

64. Which of the following is correct about questions teachers can ask students to help them learn about making inferences?
    a. Asking students information they used to make an inference helps them understand source types.
    b. Asking students what the inference is that they have made is unnecessary, as they already know it.
    c. Asking students if their thinking was valid making inferences is less important than that they think.
    d. Asking students if they should change their thinking shows their first inference is usually not valid.

65. How are games wherein children try to solve riddles related to inferential thinking?
    a. Riddles involve induction or deduction as parts of inferential thinking.
    b. Riddles involve merely guessing rather than using inferential thinking.
    c. Riddles involve inductive reasoning but not using inferential thinking.
    d. Riddles involve deductive reasoning, but not any inferential thinking.

66. Of the following learning objectives involving data analysis for pre-K through Grade 2, which is most likely to have few or no activities that are age-appropriate for pre-K and kindergarten ages?
    a. To pose questions and collect data regarding familiar objects and everyday situations
    b. To sort various objects by their properties and categorize them accordingly in groups
    c. To represent data using line graphs, bar graphs, picture graphs, charts, and timelines
    d. To put objects on table/floor graphs by property and say the group with most/fewest

Social Studies

67. Which of the following correctly shows the chronological progress in EC development of five levels of self-awareness?
    a. Identification, self-consciousness, differentiation, situation, permanence
    b. Situation, differentiation, self-consciousness, permanence, identification
    c. Self-consciousness, identification, differentiation, permanence, situation
    d. Differentiation, situation, identification, permanence, self-consciousness

68. In developing self-awareness, which of these can infants take relatively the longest to achieve?
    a. Showing eye-hand coordination by systematically reaching for and touching things
    b. Telling apart video of themselves from video of others doing the exact same things
    c. Using their sitting, posture, and balance levels to regulate their reaching for things
    d. Telling videos of them apart from video of other babies dressed in the same things

69. In the early development of interpersonal relationships, which do children typically do first?
    a. Learn autonomy and respect for others' autonomy
    b. Learn to have trust in their parents or other adults
    c. Learn to engage in make-believe and pretend play
    d. Learn all three of these elements at the same time

70. What is accurate regarding popular conflict resolution approaches for young children?
    a. EC conflict mediation steps are similar to the steps of adult conflict mediation.
    b. Adults should listen to emotions children express but should not say anything.
    c. Adults should gather information about a conflict but not talk directly about it.
    d. Suggesting possible conflict solutions should be done by an adult, not children.

71. According to psychologist Diana Baumrind, which of the parenting styles she identified is the ideal?
    a. Authoritarian
    b. Authoritative
    c. Uninvolved
    d. Permissive

72. According to family systems theory, which statement is accurate regarding family boundaries?
    a. Disengaged families have more restricted/closed boundaries.
    b. Enmeshed families place a greater value upon independence.
    c. Disengaged families are more open to considering new input.
    d. Enmeshed families have looser and more flexible boundaries.

73. Which of the following is/are accurate about individualistic vs. collectivist orientations of some world cultures?
    a. Latin American and African cultures are more often individualistic.
    b. Individualism is less common in Canadian and Australian cultures.
    c. Native American and Asian cultures are typically more collectivist.
    d. European and North American cultures tend to have more collectivism.

74. What accurately reflects acculturation vs. assimilation?
    a. Ethnic groups' uniting to form a new culture is acculturation.
    b. A dominant culture's absorbing other cultures is assimilation.
    c. Assimilation is when cultures adopt traits from other cultures.
    d. When two or more cultures virtually fuse, this is assimilation.

75. Of the following, what is most accurate about how cultural expression influences human behavior?
    a. African-American culture has historically developed a strong oral tradition.
    b. Latin American culture has not influenced North American music or dance.
    c. Recent Asian immigrants immediately adopt American family organization.
    d. European-American policy has not affected Native American tribal culture.

76. Which statement is correct regarding cultural variances in parents' reading to children in America?
    a. Different cultural values account for all variation in parents reading to children.
    b. The primary source of variation in reading to children is parental finance limits.
    c. Parental literacy levels in L1 and L2 are the main contributors to the variations.
    d. Time, access, tradition, personal experience, and all the above cause variances.

77. Among the following, which is correct regarding some essential geography concepts?
    a. An example of absolute location is urban vs. rural land prices.
    b. Relative location equals the latitude and longitude of a place.
    c. Product and land prices are affected by geographical distance.
    d. Achievability relates to surface conditions and never changes.

78. On a geographical map, which of the following requires using a ratio to interpret?
    a. The key or legend
    b. The compass rose
    c. The scale of miles
    d. The lines in a grid

79. The interdependence of rural and urban regions on one another for their materials and products is an example of which of the following geographical concepts?
    a. Interaction
    b. Area Differentiation
    c. Both (A) and (D)
    d. Spatial Interrelatedness

80. How are graphs used to fulfill different functions?
    a. Circle graphs/pie charts show part sizes of a whole.
    b. Line graphs are best for showing relative quantities.
    c. Bar graphs are best for showing change across time.
    d. Trends show better in number columns than graphs.

81. Which of the following is accurate regarding chronological thinking in studying history?
    a. Middle school students should be able to analyze patterns of historical succession.
    b. Chronological thinking is necessary to see cause-and-effect relationships in history.
    c. Students should not be expected to interpret data from timelines until high school.
    d. Teachers should avoid using narratives to instruct younger students in chronology.

82. What is a correct reason for laws and rules that can be used to help young children understand important concepts of civics?
    a. Laws and rules punish rather than identify unacceptable citizen behaviors.
    b. Laws and rules interfere with the ability of citizens to have responsibilities.
    c. Laws and rules make society and life more predictable, orderly, and secure.
    d. Laws and rules grant greater powers to persons with positions of authority.

83. Of the following, which applies to EC activities that can help teach civics?
    a. Children's literature promotes literacy rather than applying to civics concepts.
    b. Situations in stories make civics concepts more real and concrete for children.
    c. Young children identify with characters in stories, distracting them from civics.
    d. Writing and revising class rules in small groups will not teach any civics ideas.

Science

84. Among these everyday activities of young children, which most helps them develop concepts of 1:1 correspondence?
   a. Seeing how many coins are in a piggy bank or children are in their group
   b. Distributing one item to each child in the group or fitting pegs into holes
   c. Dividing up objects into piles by their types or by having the same shape
   d. Transferring sand/rice/water among various container shapes and sizes

85. When young children build structures from blocks and then knock them down or take them apart, which of these science concepts are they learning?
   a. Concepts of shape
   b. Concepts of weight
   c. Part-whole relations
   d. Temporal sequences

86. In the scientific process, which skill do children employ most when they see patterns and meaning in the results of experiments they make?
   a. Measurement
   b. Classification
   c. Inferences
   d. Prediction

87. To teach early physics concepts, an EC teacher gives students an activity of rolling balls down ramps. The teacher asks them questions like what would happen if one ramp were longer or higher; if two different sizes of ramps were used; if they started two balls rolling down a ramp at the same time, etc. Which skills in the scientific process do the children use during this activity?
   a. Observation and communication
   b. They use every one of these skills.
   c. Skills of inference and prediction
   d. Measurements and comparisons

88. Which of these orders steps of the scientific method in the correct sequence?
   a. Formulate a hypothesis; ask a question; design and conduct an experiment; report the results; decide if the hypothesis is true or false
   b. Ask a question; formulate a hypothesis; design and conduct an experiment; decide if the hypothesis is true or false; report the results
   c. Design and conduct an experiment; ask a question; formulate a hypothesis; decide if the hypothesis is true or false; report the results
   d. Formulate a hypothesis; decide if the hypothesis is true or false; design and conduct an experiment; ask a question; report the results

89. Which states of matter are fluids?
   a. Solids are.
   b. (C) and (D)
   c. Liquids are.
   d. Gases are.

90. Which of the following is true about noble gases?
   a. They comprise half of the known elementary gases.
   b. They are compound gases with more than one atom.
   c. They are active rather than inert like other gases are.
   d. They include the gases hydrogen, oxygen, and ozone.

91. What is correct regarding the reflection of light?
   a. The law of reflection applies only to smooth surfaces.
   b. The law of reflection applies to every type of surface.
   c. The scattering of light prevents reading at any angles.
   d. The smooth surface of paper stops the scattering of light.

92. When light passes between different transparent media, its speed is changed by the change in medium and it is refracted, as when a straw in a glass of water seems to break or bend at the waterline. The amount that a medium slows down the speed of light is the:
   a. Normal line.
   b. Wavelength.
   c. Refraction index.
   d. Angle of refraction.

93. Which of the following is true about how light is absorbed?
   a. The sky is blue because the atmosphere reflects only blue wavelengths.
   b. The sky is blue because the atmosphere absorbs only blue wavelengths.
   c. Glass is transparent to all of the frequencies of light within the spectrum.
   d. Wood, metal, and other opaque materials reflect all wavelengths of light.

94. Of the three ways that heat is transferred, which occur(s) within our atmosphere and also when we boil water?
   a. Radiation
   b. Convection
   c. Conduction
   d. All of these

95. What is true about magnetism?
   a. Opposite poles of magnets repel one another.
   b. The like poles of a magnet attract one another.
   c. Magnets must touch to attract or repel each other.
   d. Compasses point north because Earth is a magnet.

96. Suppose you see a rock on the ground and kick it into the air. It travels some distance and then falls back to the ground. The rock's sitting on the ground initially is explained by Newton's ____ Law of Motion. The rock's reaction of traveling when you kick it is explained by Newton's ____ Law of Motion. The rock's traveling for however long it does is explained by Newton's ____ Law of Motion. The rock's falling back to the ground is explained by Newton's ____ Law of Motion.
   a. First; Third; First; Second
   b. First; Second; Third; First
   c. Second; Third; First; Third
   d. Third; Second; First; First

97. Which of the following is correct regarding how objects produce sound and how we hear it?
   a. Sound is something that causes vibrations in the air.
   b. Sound waves are vibrations disturbing media like air.
   c. Sound causes vibrations in the air but not in the ear.
   d. Sound is the same energy type in the ear and brain.

98. Which of the following planets in the solar system is the farthest away from the sun?
   a. Mercury
   b. Neptune
   c. Jupiter
   d. Saturn

99. What is true about erosion on the surface of the Earth?
   a. Erosion causes rock, dirt, and sand to disappear from the Earth.
   b. Erosion causes rock, dirt, and sand to change form and location.
   c. Erosion occurs via mechanical processes, but not chemical ones.
   d. Erosion breaks down rather than building up areas of the Earth.

100. Among the three types of rock on the Earth, which one is formed out of the other two?
   a. Sedimentary
   b. Metamorphic
   c. Igneous rock
   d. All three are.

101. Of the following life forms, which has a life cycle featuring an incomplete metamorphosis?
   a. Butterflies
   b. Dragonflies
   c. Amphibians
   d. Mammals

102. In terms of relationships between organisms and between organisms and their environments, the relationship between termites and the bacteria in their digestive systems is classified as:
   a. Parasitic
   b. Ecological
   c. Mutualistic
   d. Commensalistic

Health and Physical Education

103. Which of the following are targeted by the 2009 American Recovery and Reinvestment Act as the primary preventable causes of disability and death?
   a. Obesity and tobacco use
   b. Alcohol and tobacco use
   c. Obesity and alcohol use
   d. Alcohol and drug abuse

104. To protect children from environmental health risks, which of the following can prevent or limit toxicity from heavy metals?
    a. Carefully choosing among which fish to eat
    b. Preparing formula and foods in cold water
    c. Preventing paint exposure in older houses
    d. All of these minimize heavy metal toxicity.

105. In the human cardiovascular system, what is the largest artery in the body?
    a. The atrium
    b. Pulmonary
    c. The aorta
    d. Vena cava

106. Which parts of the human musculoskeletal system are NOT types of connective tissue?
    a. Ligaments
    b. Tendons
    c. Cartilage
    d. Joints

107. In the human central nervous system, what is correct about the sympathetic and parasympathetic nervous systems?
    a. The sympathetic stimulates organ muscles; the parasympathetic stimulates heartbeat.
    b. One is in the voluntary nervous system; the other is in the autonomic nervous system.
    c. Both the sympathetic and parasympathetic are parts of the voluntary nervous system.
    d. Both the sympathetic and parasympathetic are part of the autonomic nervous system.

108. In the human digestive system, which of the following is a part of the large intestine?
    a. The colon
    b. The ileum
    c. The jejunum
    d. The duodenum

109. In the human body, what kind of organ is the pancreas?
    a. It is an exocrine gland only.
    b. It is an endocrine gland only.
    c. Neither endocrine nor exocrine
    d. It is both endocrine and exocrine.

110. Regarding physical, emotional, and social factors that influence personal physical health, which of the following is true?
    a. Anxiety and depression cause sleep and diet problems but not cardiovascular troubles.
    b. Stress and family dysfunction cause emotional problems, not physical illness.
    c. Air pollution can aggravate asthma but is not actually found to cause asthma.
    d. People can overeat and be overweight, and yet still suffer from malnutrition.

111. Which of these is most closely linked with symptoms resembling those of ADHD in children?
    a. Skipping breakfast
    b. Often missing meals
    c. Deficiencies in iron
    d. Protein deficiencies

112. Of the following motor skills, which do babies or toddlers typically develop the latest?
    a. Play "pattycake"
    b. Pull up to stand
    c. Jumping in place
    d. The pincer grasp

113. During which period do children's motor skills develop the fastest?
    a. Birth to 2 years
    b. From 2–6 years
    c. From 6–8 years
    d. None of these

114. Which of these infant reflexes normally disappears at the latest ages?
    a. Babinski reflex
    b. Stepping reflex
    c. Grasping reflex
    d. The tonic reflex

115. Of the following, which statement is correct about cephalocaudal and proximodistal development?
    a. Cephalocaudal means from near to far; proximodistal means from head to tail.
    b. Control of the arms develops in babies before control of the fingers develops.
    c. Cephalocaudal and proximodistal development after birth differ from in utero.
    d. Babies develop control of their legs before they develop control of their heads.

116. Which of these is most accurate about opportunities that physical activity provides?
    a. Children develop self-efficacy as well as self-esteem through effort and perseverance.
    b. Children develop their language skills younger than motor skills to express themselves.
    c. Children develop physical skills through games and sports but do not learn social skills.
    d. Children enjoy interacting socially in games but do not naturally seek physical activity.

117. What have some researchers found about physical exercise relative to school performance?
    a. Children who sit more can focus attention better than those who are more active.
    b. Children who are more physically active do better on standardized academic tests.
    c. Children who study more have better working memory than more active children.
    d. Children who exercise more do not show as good problem-solving skills as others.

Creative and Performing Arts

118. If a class curriculum involves a unit on space travel, which of these would thematically integrate an art activity for the students?
    a. Painting portraits of their classmates
    b. Constructing models of rocket ships
    c. Exploring materials all in one color
    d. Using art to express their feelings

119. Which of these is an example of art produced to serve a physical purpose?
    a. Depression photography the FSA commissioned
    b. The "Last Supper" painting by Leonardo Da Vinci
    c. Raku pottery bowls for Japanese tea ceremonies
    d. Some of the satirical artworks of Francisco Goya

120. Among the artistic processes of creating, performing, and responding, in which order do these steps of the creating process occur?
    a. Imagining; planning; evaluating and refining; presenting
    b. Planning; imagining; presenting; evaluating and refining
    c. Evaluating and refining; planning; presenting; imagining
    d. Presenting; imagining; evaluating and refining; planning

121. Which of the following is accurate regarding shape, form, and value in visual art?
    a. Shapes in art are always positive and defined by outlines.
    b. Biomorphic shapes in art are shapes which are geometric.
    c. Value in visual works of art is dependent upon the colors.
    d. Form has mass in 3-D art but appears to have it in 2-D art.

122. Which of the following is a secondary color?
    a. Yellow
    b. Green
    c. Blue
    d. Red

123. What is true about complementary colors?
    a. They are next to one another on the color wheel.
    b. They are opposite each other on the color wheel.
    c. When mixed in equal amounts, they create black.
    d. Two complementary colors are each cool or warm.

124. In music, the frequencies of individual sound waves equate to:
    a. Pitch.
    b. Tempo.
    c. Rhythm.
    d. Harmony.

125. What is true about texture in the visual arts?
    a. Texture must be felt, so it can exist only in 3-D artwork.
    b. Texture refers to rough or smooth, but not wet or dry.
    c. Texture in visual art may be real or it may be an illusion.
    d. Texture means how art feels, rather than how it looks.

126. Of the following, which is correct about balance in visual art?
    a. Balance by definition must always be symmetrical.
    b. Balance in art can be symmetrical or asymmetrical.
    c. Balance must be physical instead of psychological.
    d. Radial balance does not feature any central point.

Answers and Explanations

Language and Literacy

1. B: Among tasks that require and teach phonological awareness, hearing sounds or phonemes within words that rhyme is the easiest of the choices given. Being able to manipulate phonemes by replacing one sound in a word with another sound to make a new word (A), e.g., changing *cat* to *hat*, is one of the hardest tasks. Being able to isolate or separate sounds in words and to classify them (C) as initial, medial, or final sounds in words is easier than manipulating them, but harder than working with rhymes. Blending phonemes and syllables, i.e., combining them into words, and segmenting or separating words into their component syllables and sounds (D) are both easier than manipulating phonemes, but harder than isolating and classifying them.

2. C: Among categories of phonological awareness activities, working with rhymes is less difficult than others. Within the rhyming category, the easiest activity for children is to identify which words they hear rhyme with each other. The second easiest rhyme activity is being able to discriminate rhyming from non-rhyming words by picking which words in a list rhyme (B). The hardest rhyme activity is creating rhymes by naming words that rhyme with a word that is given (A). Therefore, these are not all equally difficult (D).

3. B: Phonics means the relationship between speech sounds or phonemes and the alphabet letters that represent those sounds. Phonics is not alphabetic knowledge (A) alone, but knowledge of how alphabet letters stand for certain speech sounds. Recognizing individual speech sounds within words (C) and being able to manipulate those speech sounds (D) are both parts of *phonemic awareness* rather than of phonics.

4. A: This is a description of the metalinguistic ability of word consciousness. The metalinguistic ability of print conventions (B) involves learning how to hold a book properly, where to start reading it, the directionality of print, and line-to-line continuity. The metalinguistic ability of print functions (C) involves learning that print can be applied for different functions and purposes, like conveying information, providing entertainment, etc. The metalinguistic ability of reading fluency (D) involves learning, via being read to by adults, how to use intonation correctly and how to read in phrases rather than single words when reading—aloud for listener comprehension and silently for reader comprehension.

5. C: The sentence is incorrect grammatically because the correct form of the verb "to be" for the third person plural subject "they" is "are," not "am." It is syntactically (A) correct because all of the words are in the correct sequence. An example of incorrect syntax would be "They are dinner out to going." The sentence is semantically (B) correct because it uses words with their correct meanings. An example of incorrect semantics would be "They are sleeping out to dinner." The sentence is morphologically (D) correct because the structure of the words used is correct. An example of incorrect morphology would be "They *aren't* going out to dinner" used to mean the same thing as "They *are* going out to dinner."

6. A: The pragmatic component of oral language development involves learning the rules for using speech that is appropriate to various social situations, including how to speak and when to speak or not speak. The phonological component (B) of oral language development involves learning the rules for putting speech sounds or phonemes into words. The semantic component (C) of oral language development involves learning the rules for combining morphemes into words (e.g.,

"book" + "s" = "books") and words into sentences to convey the meanings intended. The syntactic component (D) of oral language development involves learning the rules for combining words in the correct sequence or order to create understandable sentences.

7. B: The One-Word stage typically begins when children are about one year old. Their utterances consist of single words, some of which are real words and some invented words, also known as idiomorphs. For example, a child may consistently use the idiomorphs "bankie" to mean his or her special security blanket. In the Cooing stage (A), infants around six weeks and older naturally begin to make vowel-like sounds as they experiment with their oral skills. In the Telegraphic stage (C), toddlers produce utterances of several words, but without any connecting function words like articles (e.g., "the" or "those"), prepositions (e.g., "on," "in," "to"); plural or possessive endings ("s") or other morphemes. For example, they may say "Daddy hat" to mean "Daddy's hat." In the Babbling stage (D), infants about 4–6 months and older begin to produce consonant-vowel combinations that they repeat, like "ba-ba-ba." By about 8–10 months old, infant babbling develops the rhythms and intonations, without the actual words, of adult speech.

8. C: The five stages of second-language acquisition, in chronological order, are Preproduction, Early Production, Speech Emergence, Intermediate Fluency, and Advanced Fluency. Preproduction involves no speech and minimal listening comprehension. In the Early Production (A) stage, children have limited English comprehension of basic and familiar words and phrases and can answer simple questions with answers of one or two words. In the Speech Emergence (B) stage, ESL children can talk in simple English sentences and have good listening comprehension, but frequently misunderstand jokes told in English. In the Intermediate Fluency (C) stage, English listening comprehension is excellent; this is the earliest stage wherein ESL students can understand jokes in English all or most of the time. By the time they reach the Advanced Fluency (D) stage, ESL students have speech production and listening comprehension akin to those of native English speakers.

9. D: The age norm for correctly pronouncing /s/ and /r/, the two most difficult phonemes for children to articulate, is around 7–8 years of age. Therefore, if a child who is 5–6 years old cannot correctly pronounce these sounds, it would be considered normal language development (C) as many children's speech mechanisms are not yet mature enough to produce them perfectly. However, in a child 9–10 years old, such misarticulations could indicate a possible articulation problem, which is often corrected fairly easily with speech therapy. Although hearing loss (A) and intellectual disability (B) are two possible sources of articulation disorders, there are many other causes. Hence, it cannot be assumed that either one is the reason for the misarticulation.

10. B: By around 18 months, children should communicate using vocalizations more than gestures. If a child this age shows marked preference for gestures over voice, this is cause for concern that his/her speech and language development may be delayed. Children normally communicate via gestures, like pointing and waving, around 12 months old and imitate adult speech sounds around 18 months. However, it is not necessarily a sign of delayed development if an 18-month-old is not speaking in words yet {(A), (C)}. While it is common for children to begin using real and invented words around 12 months, there is a range for normal development. Parents should only be concerned if their child above 2 years old does not spontaneously produce words. It is normal if an 18-month-old can speak, but parents do not understand most of it (D): they should be able to understand about 50–70 percent of a 2-year-old's speech, about 75–80 percent of a 3-year-old's speech, most of a 4-year-old's speech, and all of a 5-year-old's speech.

11. D: The alphabetic principle is the concept that printed letters and letter combinations correspond to speech sounds. In order to learn the sounds that alphabet letters represent, children must first know the names of the letters. First they learn letter names, then they learn the shapes of the letters (A), and then they learn the sounds indicated by the letters (B). They learn each of these in sequence rather than all at the same time (C).

12. D: English uses multiple pronunciations of the same letters and letter combinations, whereas Spanish does not; this makes learning English more complicated for Spanish-speaking students. Another consideration is that Spanish letters correspond more consistently to their sounds than in English. Spanish has *fewer* total vowel sounds than English, not more (A). English is taught by individual phonemes and their letters, whereas Spanish is taught by syllables, not vice versa (B). Certain consonant clusters, like /sk/, /sp/, and /st/, are found at the beginnings of English words, but only follow an "e" in Spanish and are never word-initial, not vice versa (C). This makes it difficult for Spanish-speaking ESLs to pronounce English words with those initial consonant clusters; they often reproduce the initial Spanish "e" (e.g., "espeak," "estart," etc.)

13. D: Numerous research investigations into preschoolers' print awareness have found that although four-year-olds typically have NOT mastered either print concepts or word concepts (A), their acquisition of many print concepts may often precede their learning of word concepts rather than vice versa (C). Research overwhelmingly shows that the print literacy skills of preschoolers DO predict how well they will read when they are older (B).

14. C: In the first stage of reading acquisition for reading their first 30–50 words, children typically learn to associate certain visual cues with specific words, e.g., the printed words "donkey" and "dog" have "tails" on their respective final "y" and "g" or the "m" in "camel" has "humps." Or they recognize the word "moon" by its pair of o's. The second stage is reading by phonetic cues, a rudimentary decoding process of recognizing the sounds of specific letters like consonants in a word, especially the initial and final letters; e.g., a child may be able to decode "giraffe" by identifying the sounds represented by the *g, r,* and *f.* The third stage is alphabetic reading, i.e., being able to recognize *all* letter-to-sound correspondences in printed words. The fourth stage is orthographic reading, i.e., being able to read all word spellings, including words with irregular spellings and pronunciations, silent letters, etc.

15. C: Research finds that children with good reading comprehension are able to summarize the text they have read and make predictions based on it. Rather than only reading text familiar within their existing knowledge (A), they are able to make connections or associations of new material to the knowledge they already have that is pertinent to the text. They are not only skilled at decoding words, but they also have good vocabularies, which *is* necessary (B) because it is exceedingly hard for readers to comprehend text if they are unable to define many of the words in it. Readers with good comprehension also do show skills in using the sentence structure (D) in the text they read to aid their reading comprehension. Many cues in sentence syntax and grammar help them rule out some meanings and confirm others.

16. B: In this example, the reader uses the context of the sentence to understand the meaning of "reeds" rather than "reads" without needing to know how each is spelled, because the former makes sense in the context while the latter does not, semantically or grammatically. The reader is not using phonics (A) because both words sound the same, and in this case both "ea" and "ee" have the same sound. The reader is not using spelling (C) because the question states that s/he is unfamiliar with seeing these words in print. The reader cannot be assumed to be using pictures (D) in this case because the question never states there are any illustrations of the text.

17. B: In children's literature, picture books represent both a genre (A), a type of book, and a format (C) that includes other different genres within it. For example, picture books can be fictional or nonfiction, narrative or expository, prose or poetry, traditional or modern, etc. Wordless storybooks have only pictures and no text; picture books have pictures and text integrated interdependently; and illustrated storybooks have primarily text, with secondary but complementary and usually plentiful pictures. Hence picture books represent both genre and format, so their representing neither (D) is incorrect.

18. A: These are all characteristics in children's books that help early literacy development. Pictures (B) help young children learn to recognize letters and words when they can see them as related to visual images familiar to them. Rhyming (C) text helps children with phonological awareness, gets their attention, and is easier for them to remember and repeat along with adults reading to them. Repetition (D) is something young children enjoy: they love to repeat familiar phrases, rhymes, chants, songs, and stories over and over, and they notably ask adults to reread the same books to them over and over again. Repetition helps children practice and remember words and linguistic patterns. It also importantly allows young children to participate in reading right away, before they can read on their own, when adults reread familiar books to them.

19. D: To find good children's literature, adults should seek books written by authors who are knowledgeable about their chosen subject matter. They should avoid books with overtly moralistic themes (A) or books that make use of gender, racial, or other stereotypes (B). Good children's literature should have believable plots, even fantasy books: if they are unbelievable (C), children will not find them any more credible than adults will. Books should also afford enjoyable listening and/or reading experiences for children.

20. D: Children with dyslexia commonly have difficulty with reading not only long words with multiple syllables, but also with reading shorter function words (e.g., "on," "in," "that," "an"). Children with dyslexia do NOT always sound out words (A). A common characteristic of dyslexia is not having or using systematic strategies like sounding out or decoding words, and instead guessing wildly at words they do not recognize. Dyslexic students often rely on sentence context to comprehend the meaning of text; hence they find single words more difficult to understand in isolation, rather than vice versa (B). Another common characteristic of students with dyslexia is that they usually score much lower on objective tests than would be consistent with their intelligence and knowledge bases (C).

21. C: Children do not necessarily have to be able to read words in order to spell them (A). In fact, once children learn how to spell certain words, they can usually then read them (B) in text. With experience, children notice basic patterns in letter combinations that form syllables, roots that many related words share in common, common word endings (e.g., *-tion, -ate*, etc.), commonly used prefixes and suffixes, etc. Knowledge of these patterns, together with the basic spelling principles and rules of their language, are prerequisites to learning to spell; hence (B) is incorrect. Once they have learned these prerequisite patterns, principles, and rules, children typically *do* infer the correct spellings of many new words when they hear them spoken (D).

22. D: Gentry (1982) identified five stages of spelling development. Children can use letters of the alphabet during the Precommunicative stage, but do not yet understand letter-to-sound correspondence. In the second, Semiphonetic stage, children first begin to understand that certain letters stand for certain sounds. In the third, Phonetic stage (C), children represent every speech sound they hear with letters—logically and systematically, albeit not always correctly (e.g., "wuz" for "was"). In the fourth, Transitional stage (A), children progress from their phonetic spellings to

the conventionally correct spellings of words—though they are still apt to make mistakes as they learn. During the fifth, final Correct stage (B), children generally use accurate spelling.

23. B: Linguistic research into preschoolers' invented spellings (i.e., phonetic spellings of words they hear before they have learned how to spell) has found that the majority of invented spellings are the same for the same words, regardless of differences among the children studied. Hence (A) is incorrect. These coinciding spelling inventions occur at too high a rate to be explained by adult influence (C) or chance (D). The researchers have thus concluded that most preschoolers have developed sufficient phonemic and phonetic awareness to recognize the phonetic characteristics of the words that they hear, even before they have learned conventional spelling.

24. B: If a child is asked to say the first sound in the word "cow" and responds by making the /k/ sound, the child has some phonemic awareness; i.e., s/he is able to recognize this single sound (phoneme) in different words and various word positions (e.g., initial in "cow," medial in "baking," final in "milk"); to distinguish it from other phonemes, and to know that the letters "k", and "c" and "ch" (in some cases) represent this sound. The child who responds with "Moo" can be said with certainty to lack phonemic awareness. Many children have normal hearing (A), know all the letters in the alphabet (C), and have normal or above normal intelligence (D), but can still lack phonemic awareness; hence this can be said with more certainty than the other possibilities.

25. D: Children go through five identified stages in writing development. Scribbling and drawing (A) is the first stage, when children explore line, form, and space as they hold crayons, etc., in their little fists. The second stage, letter-like forms and shapes (D), is when they first realize that meanings are represented through written symbols. Their drawings and "writings" now include circles, squares, and other shapes, randomly placed with minimal spatial orientation. It is common in this stage for children to write figures and then ask their parents what they "say." In the third stage (B), children start to write real letters. They usually produce written consonants first, without awareness of letter-to-sound correspondence; they develop this gradually. They enjoy writing their own name initials. In the fourth, letters and spaces stage (C), children understand the concept of words, space words correctly, and use 1:1 word correspondence. They can write initial and final word phonemes, and experiment with constructing and punctuating sentences. The fifth stage is conventional writing and spelling.

26. A: Literacy research shows that reading and writing development have mutual benefits: improving one improves the other, and vice versa. Researchers find that children's capacity to learn is increased by increases in *both* reading and writing skills (B). Educational researchers have also found that to write well, children must have instruction; it is not a skill set that comes naturally to them (C). It is not true that having good writing skills enables the writer to meet any purpose or audience using the same single writing style (D): a part of learning writing skills is learning the ability to vary one's style and write in different genres to suit different purposes (e.g., to persuade, to inform, to amuse, or to express ideas and feelings) and different intended audiences (e.g., using different language, tone, and references that are relevant to and appeal to different readers).

27. C: The POWER strategy, one popular writing instruction model, features five steps. Planning, the first step, is one many students tend to neglect: they simply plunge in and start writing without any pre-writing work. Planning includes choosing a topic: teachers help students complete a Yes/No checklist about whether a good topic was chosen, and also help them research and read about the topic, consider information readers would want, and write down all topic-related ideas. In Organization (A), the second step, teachers help students see if they grouped related ideas, chose the best ones for the composition, and logically numbered/ordered them. The third step is writing,

including all ideas in full sentences and getting help as needed from texts, teachers, or classmates. The fourth step, Editing (D), includes reading the first draft, marking parts s/he likes and those s/he might change, and reading it to a classmate to hear feedback. The fifth step, rewriting (B), involves making needed changes, correcting mechanics, and the final draft.

28. C: Clay's (1993) rating scale for emergent writing skills in children assesses three areas: language level, message quality, and directional principles. Language level (A) includes progressing from letters to words to phrases to sentences, to punctuated stories, to stories including two themes and more than one paragraph. Message Quality (C) includes understanding the concepts of signs or symbols and message communication, copying messages, repeating sentence patterns, writing one's own ideas, and successful composition. Directional Principles (B) includes learning the correct directionality and spacing in writing text. Since (C) is correct, (D) is incorrect.

29. D: A traditional teacher practice was to pay more attention to composition length, appearance, word usage, and spelling—i.e., form—more than organization or content—i.e., function. Today, teachers are more inclined to attend to function more than in the past (A). However, flawed form still makes negative first impressions on both teachers and other readers, even when a composition is otherwise effective in conveying its message(s). Teachers should judge both form and function equally (B), which they did not tend to do historically. Hence (C) is incorrect.

30. D: If a student's handwriting is illegible, readers will not be able to access the content expressed. While all writing conventions are important, the very first thing to prevent readers from perceiving the content of a composition is whether they can read it. Errors in capitalization (A) will make a composition look uninformed and/or unedited; errors in sentence construction (B) can imply substandard writing skills and/or lack of editing, and can interfere with meaning (as with dangling participles, misplaced modifiers, etc.); and errors in punctuation (C) can also interfere with meaning, as well as making the writing harder to read and understand. While today's computer technology can eliminate handwriting problems for many students and leave only typing errors (despite spell-check software, which will *not* make typing perfect without human attention), younger children must still learn to write by hand, and students are still frequently required to submit handwritten work.

31. A: This version is correctly punctuated because it is a compound-complex sentence, consisting of two independent clauses and a dependent/subordinate (relative) clause. Independent clauses should be separated by a semicolon. In (B) and (D), the two independent clauses have no punctuation separating them, creating a run-on sentence; additionally, (B) has an incorrect comma between the first independent clause and the subordinating conjunction "that," which introduces the relative clause. (If "that" were omitted, it would be correct with or without the comma.) Version (C) incorrectly separates the independent clauses with a comma instead of a semicolon.

32. C: The correct spelling of this adverb is "similarly," from the adjective "similar" meaning like, akin to, or resembling. (There is a word "simular" from the same Latin root, meaning one who simulates or dissembles; however, it is archaic [no longer used] and moreover is a noun. There is no such word as "simularly.") Simulacrum (A) is correctly spelled; it is a noun meaning a representation, image, or trace of something real. Stimulate (B) is spelled correctly; it is a verb meaning to activate or excite. Simulate (D) also has the correct spelling; it is from the same root as "simulacrum" and the archaic "simular"—see above (the Latin *simulare*, to simulate or imitate).

33. B: This sentence correctly capitalizes the place name of Washington, D.C., a proper noun. The word "president" is incorrectly capitalized in (A): it should only be capitalized when used as a proper noun, e.g., "President Obama." But when a civil title is used instead of a name as it is here, it is not capitalized. The word "south" is incorrectly capitalized in (C). Compass directions are not capitalized, as in "coming south" or "going south." They are capitalized only when referring to actual regions, as in "We live in the South." The words "science" and "math" are incorrectly capitalized in (D). Academic subjects are not capitalized. It is correct to capitalize "English" because it is derived from the proper noun "England." *Specific* titles of classes or courses, like "Elementary Algebra" or "Math 101" should be capitalized, but general nouns like "science" and "math" should not.

34. D: Many researchers have studied children's temporary invented spelling and found that when children are encouraged to use invented spelling, compared to children not encouraged to use invented spelling, they write substantially longer and more complex stories rather than shorter ones (A); and their scores on both spelling and reading posttests are significantly higher than their pretest scores. The researchers believe these findings mean that children develop *better* skills of word analysis through using invented spelling (B), likely via more practice with and application of letter-to-sound correspondences in writing. This research belies worries that invented spellings will interfere with children's subsequent correct spelling (C).

35. A: According to educational and literacy experts, teachers can sustain young children's interest and enthusiasm for writing by providing them with a variety of different writing activities rather than letting them get bored by always assigning the same kinds of writing tasks. Teachers can also set up "writing corners" in their classrooms including writing contributions from children and teachers that demonstrate a variety of kinds and styles of writing. Adults and children alike enjoy tasks that are fun, so teachers *should* offer these (B) to make writing enjoyable rather than a chore. Experts advise teachers to transcribe what young children dictate, and have children practice sounding out and spelling words as they say them. They also *do* recommend that teachers deliberately make some transcription errors for children to spot and correct (C). Another recommendation is to let young children each take turns contributing one sentence to a daily class newsletter; assigning each child to write an entire one alone (D) is an inappropriate demand for most young children/beginning writers.

36. B: Writers who teach writing find that students do not work as hard on writing only their teacher will see (A) as on writing that will be posted in the classroom. They find when students know they will read what they write aloud in class presentations, they are more motivated to do their best, not inhibited (C). Even home-schooled students can have audiences (D): parents can display their children's writing on refrigerators, walls, bulletin boards, etc.; schedule weekly recital nights when every family member reads what they wrote during the week; work with children to compose family newsletters; form writing clubs with other home-schooling families; compile year-end/semester-end books of their work; attend annual writing conventions with children and present their books; make blogs or web pages; find pen pals for children; and encourage children to write to their celebrity heroes and to local newspaper editors.

Mathematics

37. C: Children are innately curious about solving everyday problems (A); hence adults can make use of this natural characteristic by asking children to offer solutions. Once a child resolves a problem, the adult should also ask them to explain how they came to their solution. Practicing problem-solving not only teaches children to think mathematically; it also expedites language

development and social skills development (B) when they work together with others. Experts advise adults not only to propose problems and ask questions about them to children, but also to have children do these things themselves (D). This gives them practice in how to think through and figure out things for themselves, as well as helping them realize that many problems have multiple and varied possible solutions.

38. A: When children engage in problem-solving activities, they develop skill with regulating their own thinking, feelings, and behaviors. These are critical to their development into mature individuals and members of society. Problem-solving also encourages children to be flexible, not rigid (B) as they consider alternate methods and solutions and experiment with them. Solving problems does not make children impatient; instead, practice in problem-solving encourages their persistence (C) with trying different approaches and repeated attempts if the first one does not succeed. Problem-solving activity does not promote dangerous risk-taking (D) in children; however, it does promote their willingness to take reasonable risks.

39. B: When adults ask children questions, give them time to think, and then attend to their answers, they help children learn to reason. Rather than analyzing and explaining children's own thought processes to them (A), adults do better allowing children to analyze their own thinking and then explain it. Children have this ability; encouraging them to use it gives them practice, developing their reasoning skills. They need these to understand and apply early math and science concepts, and to negotiate everyday life. Rather than tell children why something is a certain way and discussing it with them (C), adults should ask children why without expecting particular answers. This allows children to think for themselves; adults should listen to their ideas. Adults should encourage children to use logic to classify things rather than doing it for them (D). While occasional examples can help get struggling children started, it is generally better if adults invite children to use their existing logical abilities.

40. D: Young children typically have not attained the cognitive development yet to be able to perform mental operations using only abstract ideas (A). However, even young children can begin to appreciate abstract concepts if these are expressed through concrete objects (B) they can touch and manipulate, and visual graphics (C) that they can see. For example, even in their toddler years, children will hold up their fingers to show how many years old they are, showing that they can understand abstractions like numbers if they have concrete things to associate them with and express them.

41. D: One excellent way that adults and children can communicate with each other about mathematics is to read children's books together that incorporate numbers with words that rhyme and are repeated. Rhyming and repetition attract young children's attention and facilitate their engagement, memory, and participation. Many good children's books also integrate numbers, promoting children's literacy and numeracy development concurrently. Another good way to communicate about math is to have conversations about math problems and concepts. It helps children clarify their own thoughts when they talk about them with *both* adults *and* peers (A). Communication about math furthers not only children's mathematical thinking, but *also* their language development, vocabularies, and early reading skills (B). Adults can help children understand math concepts by using diagrams, symbols, *and* words and pictures, which are all effective (C).

42. A: Educational experts agree that to develop children's early math and science skills, adults should ask questions that guide children to solve problems on their own rather than telling them the "right answer." Experts also advise adults to disregard age/grade levels (B) in giving math

games and problems to young children, because children are versatile enough to consider any scenario they can mentally visualize. Even at toddler ages, children can handle division problems, so adults should not avoid these (C). A toddler's solution to dividing three cookies between two people will be efficient, albeit not necessarily equitable. It is better to use familiar objects in story problems with young children. Rather than distracting them from the problem (D), children's favorite foods, toys, pets, etc., facilitate their addressing the problem because they are easiest for children to visualize, and are the most natural and appealing topics to incorporate into solving problems.

43. B: One way that teachers can help young children connect mathematics to real everyday life is to describe children's typical activities to them using mathematical vocabulary words. This enables children to realize how they routinely perform mathematical operations every day. Formal math instruction (A) too often results in young children's view of math as an isolated set of rules that they do not apply for problem-solving in their everyday lives. Teachers can bridge formal and intuitive mathematics by using manipulatives in math that are familiar to children rather than novel (C). Familiar objects help children relate math to life. Similarly, when teachers introduce children to new math concepts, illustrating them using examples related to children's real-life experiences rather than original but unfamiliar examples (D) will make the concepts more relevant to them personally—and thereby more understandable as well as more meaningful.

44. A: Pouring liquid into differently sized and shaped containers is an activity that is easy and fun to do. It helps develop young children's ability to measure (B) amounts of liquid; to achieve what Piaget termed conservation (C) of liquid volume when they realize that an amount remains the same despite being transferred to a different shape or size of container; and to estimate (D) how much liquid will fit into various containers, which will hold the most and the least, etc. In addition, this game helps develop children's spatial sense. Such activities help children connect math to everyday life.

45. D: When young children begin to play "make-believe" or "pretend," they are demonstrating that they have acquired representation skills, i.e., using one thing to stand for/represent another. This occurs at early ages; hence (A) is incorrect. More examples of how children use representation skills include counting on their fingers (B)—fingers are concrete objects they use to represent numbers; drawing pictures (C)—pictures are themselves symbolic representations of real objects and people; and making marks to keep tallies (D) or counts of objects, people, turns taken, game scores, etc.

46. D: Each of these choices is an example of how a different math process skill can be applied during children's typical preschool activities. With a child who is sorting toys by color, when the teacher describes this activity to the child as classification (A), the teacher is connecting the informal activity with an application of mathematical vocabulary. When the teacher asks the child to explain how s/he is dividing up the toys (B), this applies the process of communication in mathematics. When the teacher asks the child once s/he is done sorting what other ways s/he could sort them (C), this applies the mathematical process skill of problem-solving.

47. B: Young children learn to count to three before they have learned all of the numbers' names; then they learn to count to five, etc. Thus, they do not know all number names before learning to count (A). Children's number sense does not equate to counting alone (C). It also includes understanding various applications of numbers—not only for describing quantities (D), but also for expressing and manipulating information, and for depicting relationships among things. Children who have developed good number sense can understand these functions as well as count, and they

can count forward and backward, dismantle and reassemble numbers, and add and subtract them. These abilities facilitate their developing all other math skills.

48. A: When adults count real environmental objects together with children and also encourage children to count things themselves, they help children understand numbers through the relevant medium of their own experiences with real-life items; to understand abstract numerical concepts through concrete objects; and to get needed practice with counting and numbers. Sorting objects by their colors, shapes, and sizes *is* also relevant to helping children develop numeracy skills (B). Adults should engage children in sorting objects by *both* difference (C) and similarity (D), which helps them understand describing quantities and relationships.

49. A: Adding and squaring, as well as subtracting, multiplying, dividing, etc., are operations; i.e., mathematical processes, procedures, or actions that involve manipulating numerical values to arrive at a new value. Numbers and fractions (B) are used in operations, but they are not operations themselves. Quotients and remainders (C) are not operations, but are respectively the results of the operation of division and the amount left over when the quotient is not an even number. Minuends and subtrahends (D) are not operations, but within the operation of subtraction are respectively the number subtracted from and the number subtracted.

50. A: Exponents like square roots and powers of numbers come before addition, subtraction, multiplication, and division in the mathematical order of operations. Calculations inside of parentheses are done before those outside of them, not vice versa (B). Multiplication and division are done before addition and subtraction, not vice versa (C). Multiplication and division have the same rank in the order; and addition and subtraction have the same rank, so (D) is incorrect. With operations having the same rank, the rule is to go from left to right in the calculation. (A mnemonic for this order is PEMDAS, i.e., Parentheses, Exponents, Multiplication and Division, Addition and Subtraction. Various phrases have been invented as acrostics for these initials, e.g., "People Everywhere Made Decisions About Sums.")

51. A: Patterns are any actions, events, movements, images, sounds, numbers, etc., that are regularly repeated; relationships are logical or reasoned associations among things. Awareness and understanding of patterns and relationships allow children to understand how objects and concepts are categorized into groups and how rhythm works (in music, dance, poetry, speech, art, etc.), as well as how to order things from smallest to biggest, etc. Being aware of and comprehending patterns and relationships not only let children understand the structures of things in reality; they also *do* allow them to predict events before they occur (B) because of the regularity of repetition in patterns and the logic in relationships. Patterns and relationships exist in geometry as well as in algebra (C) and other branches of mathematics, and also in art and music (D).

52. B: Adults can help prepare young children for future content math by giving them hands-on activities involving identifying and creating patterns and relationships. For example, adults can help children identify patterns in fabric prints, and also in art (A) like paintings, drawings, sculpture, etc. They can give children differently colored beads to string into different patterns. When young children dance to music, adults can help them identify patterns in their own movements and those of others; they need not worry about teaching, learning, or analyzing any complex dance steps (C) to do this. With arranging beads and other colored objects into patterns and identifying their relationships, alternating two colors 1:1 is NOT all they can do (D): they can progress, as children become able, to more complex patterns, e.g., 3 of one color, one of the other; 3/2/3/1/, etc. They can also add more colors to alternate and make more complex variations of how many of each color are used, and so forth.

53. A: The concept of change is naturally more familiar to young children than the concepts of Part-Whole (B) and Comparison (C). For example, when something is added to or taken away from a quantity of objects, children more readily notice that a change has taken place before they understand the concept that pieces can be parts of a larger whole, or that one thing is different from another in quantity or kind. Once young children can see the changes in value wrought by quantitative increases or decreases, they will be able to represent the relationships visually through drawing, e.g., making pictures of the concrete objects used within pre-printed boxes or cells provided. Since (A) is correct, (D) is incorrect.

54. C: With young children, it is best to start with concrete objects that they can see, touch, and manipulate as these are easiest for them to engage with and understand. For example, teachers can use marbles or other small objects that they can use to see what values they get by adding and subtracting different numbers of them (e.g.: "You have three marbles here. If I give you one more, how many do you have now?"). When children have attained comfort with this step, then teachers can have them draw pictures of the marbles inside of boxes to illustrate the concept. When children have mastered this, teachers can eventually transition them from pictures of marbles, to writing the parts of the equation as numbers (e.g., 3 + 1 = 4), and then finally to understanding this concept as an abstraction. Young children will come to understand the concept better through this progression than being hit with all three levels at the same time (D).

55. A: After adults tell young children the names of geometric shapes they are looking at, adults should thereafter ask children to tell them these names the next time. Then they should ask children to describe different shapes. Then they can ask children to use their fingers to trace existing drawings of shapes, and draw different shapes in the air with their fingers. Finally, they can ask children to make their own drawings of the shapes.

56. B: It makes it easier for very young children to understand geometric concepts when adults provide them with concrete objects (A) that they can touch and move with their own hands. Very young children will also find it easier and more enjoyable to learn about geometric shapes to incorporate them into their normal everyday activities (C). For example, adults can cut children's sandwiches into various shapes, and then let the children arrange them to fit together and rearrange them to create new and different patterns. Using things that are familiar and pleasant to young children enhances their engagement and comprehension. Adults can also enhance infants' and toddlers' development of spatial sense by letting them play (supervised) in, on, under, around, and through things like large appliance cartons, furniture, etc.

57. A: For young children, measurement is not only a way to quantify the sizes of physical objects (B) or amounts of time (C). It can help children not only understand the sizes of different objects, but *also* understand how to compare the sizes of different objects (D), which helps them understand relationships. Moreover, measurement enables children to see relationships not only in object comparison as an isolated exercise, but throughout their everyday lives and activities, and with all objects and things they encounter in real life.

58. B: Young children often spontaneously use familiar objects to express measurements before they have learned standardized measures (e.g., "He is four teddy bears tall" or "You will be home in one *Sesame Street* [1 hour], not one *SpongeBob* [1/2 hour]"). Adults should encourage rather than discourage this practice, which makes the concept of measurement understandable and relevant to them. Children will learn standard measuring units soon enough, but when they are younger there is no need to force them to learn these immediately (A). When children help with activities like

grocery shopping, cooking, gardening, sewing, carpentry, etc., it will not make their participation less enjoyable to discuss measurement with them (C). Children enjoy helping parents with everyday "grown-up" tasks, and hence enjoy learning about processes involved in accomplishing them, like measuring sizes, amounts, and times. When children use their own measurement units, adults can also make use of this natural behavior by applying it themselves (D) so young children understand what they are saying about measurements.

59. A: When adults ask young children simple questions, e.g., "Who can hold their breath longer?" or "Who can stand on one foot longer?"; this helps children learn to compare lengths of time through concrete physical actions they can understand. EC experts find it appropriate for adults to talk about minutes (e.g., "You may play for five minutes longer") even before children understand references to numbers of minutes (B), because when adults repeat such references over time, it will eventually help them realize the concept of the passage of time. It *is* also instructive to tell children how long their everyday activities took (C) to familiarize them with the concept of amounts of time. Terms like yesterday, today, and tomorrow represent abstract concepts which young children typically do not understand (D); until they do, adults can instead use more concrete frames of reference, e.g., "after lunch," "before bedtime," "when you wake up in the morning," etc.

60. A: Piaget demonstrated through experiments with very young children that they cannot yet perform logical or mathematical mental operations like dividing a whole into parts. They focus on only one aspect or property of an object rather than multiple properties; Piaget named this *centration.* When children in Piaget's Preoperational stage see several pieces of an apple, they see the total number of pieces rather than their sizes and assume several pieces equal more than one whole apple. Therefore they do not yet understand the part-whole concept {(B), (D)}, even if they can use concrete objects (C). Children in Piaget's Concrete Operations stage, around elementary school age, can understand these concepts as long as they are accompanied by concrete objects. They cannot understand them abstractly without concrete examples until Piaget's stage of Formal Operations, around the preteen to teen ages.

61. C: When the teacher lets children choose their favorite colors of stickers, they are getting practice for the future collection of data. When they match their sticker colors to corresponding colors on a piece of poster board, they are getting practice in the future organization of data. And when they see their and the other children's stickers placed on this poster as a chart that everybody can see, they are getting practice for their future display of data they have collected and organized. Identifying sticker shapes (A) is more relevant to learning figure properties. Guessing how many stickers of each color were chosen (B) is more relevant to practice in predicting probabilities. Choosing stickers as rewards for something until they accumulate enough to receive a larger reward (D) is more relevant to a token economy, used in behaviorism to increase the incidence of desired behaviors and decrease undesired ones.

62. A: According to the National Council of Teachers of Mathematics (NCTM)'s standards for students in pre-kindergarten through grade 2, children in this age range should be able to draw upon their experience to identify whether given events are "likely" or "unlikely" to occur. Being able to propose predictions and justify them based on data they gather (B); to collect and analyze data, draw conclusions about the data, and justify those conclusions using those data (C); and to design studies to investigate inferences or predictions they make (D) are all standards that the NCTM designates for students in grades 3 through 5.

63. C: One simple model to teach children about making inferences includes the following assumptions: (1.) In order to get answers to our questions, we must look for clues. Therefore (A) is

incorrect. (2.) When we find clues, we must combine them with what we already know from experience and/or reading. Thus (B) is incorrect. (3.) When seeking answers to questions, we must realize there can be more than one right answer. Hence (D) is incorrect. (4.) We must be able to support the inferences that we make (C).

64. A: Experts (cf. Marzano, 2010) recommend questions for teachers to ask students to help them learn about making inferences. Asking students what inference they have made *is* advised because this helps them realize if they have just inferred something by supplying information they did not present directly. Students just learning about inference do not necessarily know when they have made an inference (B). Asking what information students based inferences on helps them understand the different information sources—e.g., their own experiences, background knowledge, or information they read in textbooks (A). The most important element of the inferential process is for students to investigate how valid their thinking was in inferring; just that they think is not more important than that they question how good their thinking was (C). Asking students whether they should change their thinking does not mean their first inference is usually invalid (D); it is a way to teach them habits of ongoing updates to their thought as they gain additional information.

65. A: Inductive reasoning moves from the specific to the general, accruing more and more clues to the answer. Deductive reasoning moves from the general to the specific, ruling out possibilities through a process of elimination to arrive at the answer. Inductive and deductive reasoning are both parts of inferential thinking; hence (C) and (D) are incorrect. Some riddles require induction, some deduction, and some need both. Thus, playing games involving riddles helps children practice inferential thinking. Riddles do not entail merely guessing (B), but require children to use what they already know and to add to that the new information they get from progressive clues.

66. C: Pre-K and Kindergarten students are less likely to be able to display data in line graphs, bar graphs, picture graphs, charts, and timelines than students in grades 1 and 2 are. Younger children can gather common found objects during everyday play and other activities (e.g., acorns, leaves, socks, toys) and then sort them and compare their similarities and differences (A). They can also sort objects (or information) according to one given property, like color, amount, shape, size, etc., and group them accordingly (B). Younger children can additionally place objects onto a table graph or floor graph according to such groupings, and then identify which category or group contains the most or fewest objects (D).

Social Studies

67. D: The first level of EC self-awareness is differentiation, wherein children realize their reflections in mirrors are making the same movements they are, and they can tell their mirror reflections apart from other people, showing differentiation of self. The second level is situation, wherein children understand that their mirror reflections are unique to the self, and that their selves, bodies, and other things are physically situated in space. The third level is identification, wherein children can identify their mirror reflections as "me." When they see a mark on their faces by looking at a mirror, they reach for their own faces rather than for the mirror image. The fourth level is permanence, wherein children realize a permanent self, recognizing themselves in photographs and videos despite their different ages, places, clothing, etc. in these records. The fifth level is self-consciousness, also called meta-self-awareness, wherein children can see the self from the perspectives of others as well as from their own.

68. B: In the early development of self-awareness, infants normally demonstrate eye-hand coordination by systematically reaching for and touching things they see by the age of 4 months (A). They regulate their reaching behaviors according to their physical sitting, posture, and balance levels by 4–6 months of age (C). They can typically tell the difference between video of themselves and of other babies dressed in identical clothing by the age of 6 months (D). They typically can tell the difference between live video of themselves and of others exactly mimicking their behaviors by the ages of 4–7 months (B).

69. B: The earliest interpersonal interactions are those between infants and their parents or caregivers. According to Erikson, when adults meet infants' needs fully and consistently, infants learn to trust adults and by extension develop an attitude of basic trust in the world. Also according to Erikson, toddlers develop autonomy, i.e., independence in making decisions and doing things. When adults consistently let toddlers develop age-appropriate autonomy, the children are more likely to develop respect for others' autonomy (A), which is essential to interpersonal development. According to Piaget and Erikson, preschoolers develop the ability for symbolic representation, wherein they can use things to stand for other things. This enables make-believe and pretend play (C), like pretending to be grown-ups, fantasy figures, etc. Their peer interactions during such play prepare children for future interpersonal interactions in life. Since children learn these things in chronological succession, (D) is incorrect.

70. A: Popular approaches to conflict resolution for early childhood ages (e.g., the HighScope program) are typically very similar in their steps to the steps used in adult conflict mediation. When adults intervene in a conflict among young children, they are advised to listen to children's feelings, and also to acknowledge these rather than not saying anything (B). Adults should not only gather information from the children about their conflict, but should also restate the problem identified by the children rather than not talking about it (C). Suggesting possible solutions is something an adult should ask the children to do themselves rather than doing it for them (D); the adult should then help the children come to an agreement about which solution they choose. Adults should follow up with support as needed.

71. B: Baumrind designated Authoritative as the ideal parenting style for combining assertiveness and forgiveness; using discipline that is supportive rather than punitive; setting rules, but also explaining reasons for rules to children; being warm, nurturing, and responsive but also setting limits and boundaries; and democratically receiving, considering, and addressing children's viewpoints rather than ignoring them. Baumrind described the Authoritarian (A) style as directive, demanding, punitive, strict, and unresponsive. These parents make rules without explaining them and are not as warm or nurturing. She described the Uninvolved (C) style as one that makes neither demands nor responses. These parents meet children's basic needs, but are otherwise detached and uncommunicative. In the extreme, they can reject or neglect children. Permissive (D) parents are warm, nurturing, responsive, and communicative, but do not set rules and limits or discipline children.

72. C: According to family systems theory, boundaries pertain to what a family includes and excludes, its limits, and its relative levels of togetherness and separation. Characteristics of disengaged families include *less* restricted or closed boundaries rather than vice versa (A); valuing independence more highly than enmeshed families do rather than vice versa (B); and being more open to considering new input (C). Characteristics of enmeshed families include having more restricted or closed boundaries than disengaged families, rather than looser and more flexible ones (D), and valuing togetherness, belonging, and loyalty more than autonomy.

73. C: Native American and Asian cultures tend to be collectivist; i.e., they value interdependence among people, relationships, and social interactions. Latin American and African cultures also are more likely to embrace collectivism, focusing on the common good more than individual achievement; thus (A) is incorrect. Individualism, however, is *more* common in Canadian and Australian cultures, not less; so (B) is incorrect. European and North American cultures also favor individual expression, self-determination, independence, uniqueness, and self-actualization; hence they are more individualistic cultures, not more collectivist, so (D) is incorrect.

74. B: When a dominant culture absorbs other cultures so that they all adopt all the behaviors of the dominant culture, this is called assimilation: the dominant culture assimilates other cultures. When different ethnic groups unite to form a new culture, this is also assimilation, not acculturation (A). The adoption by one culture of some of another culture's traits is acculturation, not assimilation (C). When two or more different cultures virtually fuse, this is also a type of acculturation rather than assimilation (D).

75. A: Historically, slave owners did not permit the African slaves they bought to learn how to read and write. Though some slaves still managed secretly to attain literacy, the majority suffered forced illiteracy and thus developed a rich oral tradition of storytelling, songs, etc., which they transmitted to succeeding generations. Latin American culture has had a significant influence on North American music and dance (B), as evidenced in the growing popularity of Latino music within North American popular music, and in the Latin division of ballroom dancing. Recent Asian immigrants do not all immediately adopt American family structures (C); when arriving in America, extended families (grandparents, aunts, uncles, cousins, etc.) are more likely to continue living together. The policies of European-American settlers have eradicated much of Native Americans' tribal culture (D); while some groups have worked hard to preserve their tribal languages, religions, music, dance, artwork, and other customs, overall much of their culture has been lost along with much of their population.

76. D: Multiple, varied factors contribute to differences in whether and how much parents in America read to their children. It is not only the values of different cultural groups in America that account for these (A). The financial limitations some parents experience (B) also contribute, as do the literacy levels of immigrant and other linguistic minority parents in both their native languages and in English as their second language (C). Additionally, some parents have limited time to read to children because of their work schedules, other family commitments, etc.; some have limited access to resources like libraries, websites, and government agencies supporting literacy due to limitations in finances, transportation, information about and/or comfort with these; some have more oral than literary cultural traditions; and some have personal experiences of not being read to in childhood but succeeding in adulthood nonetheless. These factors and the others named above all combine to contribute to variations in reading to children among American families (D).

77. C: One geographical concept is distance. For example, product prices are affected by the cost of transportation, which in turn is affected by how far away raw materials are from the factories that process them, and prices for land closer to highways are higher than for land farther away from them. Location is another geography concept. Absolute location is determined by a place's latitude and longitude, not land prices (A). Relative location is determined by a region's changing characteristics, which surrounding areas can influence; one example is that land costs more in urban than rural areas. Relative location is not determined by latitude and longitude (B). Achievability is related to the accessibility of a geographical area; for example, villages with surrounding forests or swamps are less accessible than those on beaches. The dependency of an

area, and hence its achievability, *does* change (D) as its technology, transportation, and economy change.

78. C: In cartography, the scale of miles on a map enables us to estimate actual distances between places. For example, a map's scale of miles may state that one inch equals 500 miles. Thus, a ratio is required to interpret this information: by measuring with a ruler, if we see that the distance on the map between two cities, states, or countries equals six inches, then we can estimate the actual distance between these locations to be 3,000 miles. The key or legend (A) on a map identifies what the different symbols and colors used in the map indicate. The compass rose (B) on a map shows north, south, east, and west directions so we can see the orientations of different places. The lines in a grid (D) on a map indicate latitudes, or parallels, which run east-west, and longitudes, or meridians, which run north-south. By finding the intersection of latitude and longitude coordinates for a given place, we can determine its absolute location.

79. C: The geographical concept of Interaction (A) refers to interdependent and mutual relationships between different geographic areas. For example, urban areas depend on the raw materials (e.g., ores from mines or plant crops) from rural areas for industrial manufacturing, and rural areas depend on urban ones both as markets for their raw materials, and for the industrial products they make. The concept of Spatial Interrelatedness (D) refers to the relationship of physical and nonphysical aspects, such as the rural and urban areas described here. The concept of Area Differentiation (B) refers to differences in aspects of regional geography, e.g., how altitude and climate influence which plants are grown, and regional influences on differences in occupations, e.g., farming or fishing.

80. A: Circle graphs, aka pie charts, divide a circular shape into segments according to the percentage or fraction of the whole represented by each value measured, e.g., the population sizes of different places or the percent of funds used by each department, function, or program in an agency. These not only make the proportions readily visual, but they also enable easier comparisons of amounts. Line graphs are best for showing change over time, not relative quantities (B). Bar graphs are best for showing relative quantities rather than changes across time (C). All these kinds of graphs are better at visually depicting trends and patterns, like increases and decreases in quantity, than number columns are (D).

81. B: In order for students to understand causal relationships among historical events and processes, they must understand chronology. Analysis of historical succession patterns is a standard expected of high school students, not middle school students (A). However, students are expected to be able to interpret data from timelines by middle school, not high school (C). To instruct younger students in chronology, teachers *should* use narratives (D); e.g., histories written in story style, biographies, and historical literature. Such materials engage younger students' attention, help them to understand the historical motivations and actions of individuals and groups, and enable them to comprehend the relationships among antecedents, actions and events, and consequences as well as temporal event sequences.

82. C: One reason for laws and rules that we can communicate to young children to help them understand important civics concepts is that they confer greater predictability, order, and security to our society and hence our lives. Another reason is that laws and rules identify for citizens which behaviors are acceptable and which are unacceptable, rather than only punishing the latter (A). Another reason is that laws and rules delegate various responsibilities to citizens, rather than interfering with these (B). An additional reason is that laws and rules *limit* the power of persons in

authority positions to prevent them from abusing their positions, rather than increasing that power (D).

83. B: Children's literature can not only be used to promote literacy and numeracy in young children; EC teachers also use it to teach civics concepts. (A) is incorrect. One reason is civics concepts become more real and concrete to young children when presented through stories whose situations children can understand (B). Another reason is young children can identify with or relate to characters in stories personally, making citizenship concepts thus delivered more relevant to them rather than distracting (C). EC teachers can also teach civics through a small-group activity wherein children write class rules, and then rewrite them more realistically (e.g., "No talking in class" becomes "Talk softly in class and listen when others talk"; "Stay in your seat" becomes "Sit down and go right to work"). This activity *will* teach civics ideas (D): through it, children come to understand judicial and legislative functions, and think about concepts like safety and fairness.

Science

84. B: When young children fit pegs into matching holes, or distribute one item to each child in their group, they are developing 1:1 correspondence concepts. When they see how many coins are in a piggy bank or how many children are in their group (A), they are developing counting concepts. When they divide objects into piles of the same type or shape (C), they are developing classification concepts. When they transfer sand, rice, water, or other substances from one container to others with different sizes and shapes (D), they are developing measurement concepts.

85. C: When building block structures and then dismantling them, children learn concepts of part-whole relations. They learn concepts of shape (A) when they realize that some objects roll away from them and others do not. They learn concepts of weight (B) when they try to lift different objects and find some are heavier and some lighter. As babies, they quickly learn concepts of temporal sequences (D) when they awaken wet and/or hungry and then their parents change and/or feed them. As toddlers, they also learn temporal concepts through playing, tiring, and sleeping.

86. C: When children conduct simple experiments and are able to see patterns and meanings in the results, they are using the scientific process skill of inference. They use the skill of measurement (A) when they quantify the various physical properties of objects, like length, width, height, weight, etc. They use the skill of classification (B) when they group objects, events, conditions, or situations according to the properties they share in common. They use the skill of prediction (D) when they apply their experiences from experimenting to form new hypotheses to test.

87. B: The activity described uses each of these skills. The children use scientific observation to note what happens when they try the different ball-ramp actions the teacher suggests (and think of themselves), and they discuss their findings with and report them to one another and the teacher (A). They use inference when they realize similarities, differences, and patterns among the different actions and what these mean, and they use prediction to answer the teacher's questions about "what would happen if..." before testing them by performing the suggested actions (C). They use measurement to calculate the height and length of the ramps, the speed at which the balls roll down them, the distance they roll, and they count the numbers of balls and ramps. And they use comparison (D) when they find the differences in the effects on speed and distance of varying ramp sizes, ramp numbers, ball numbers, etc.

88. B: The first step in the scientific method is to ask a research question to which one wants to find an answer. Asking questions is also a natural behavior of children. The second step is to formulate a hypothesis, an educated guess as to the question's answer. The next steps, designing and conducting an experiment, are informed by the specific hypothesis and will test whether it is true or false. The experimenter decides if the hypothesis has been proven true or false by the results of the experiment. The final step is reporting the results and one's conclusions about them to others. Making guesses or predictions, testing them, and communicating the results to others are also natural behaviors to children; therefore, young children can readily learn the steps of the scientific method with some astute EC teacher guidance.

89. B: Both liquids (C) and gases (D) are fluids. They share certain properties, e.g., not keeping any shape and spreading indefinitely outside of containers. Solids (A) are not fluids because they have specific atomic structures that are crystalline or three-dimensional, and specific melting points. Solids have the most cohesive molecules; gases have the least cohesive molecules; and liquids have molecules in between solids and gases in cohesion.

90. A: Of all gases, elementary gases are those made up of only one chemical element. Of the twelve known elementary gases, six are noble gases. Noble gases are NOT compound gases (B); they are composed of single atoms. Noble gases ARE inert gases, not active (C); they do not easily form compounds with other gases because their oxidation value is 0, and they have the most electrons possible in their outer shells (8 in each noble gas except helium, which has 2), so they are stable gases. Hydrogen, oxygen, and ozone are elementary gases, but NOT noble gases (D). The other elementary gases that are not noble gases are chlorine, fluorine, and nitrogen. The noble gases are argon, helium, krypton, neon, radon, and xenon.

91. A: In physics, the law of reflection is: "The angle of incidence equals the angle of reflection." In other words, light bounces off a surface at the same angle that it strikes that surface. However, this only applies to smooth surfaces (A), like mirror glass. It does not apply to all surfaces (B). When light strikes a rough surface, it is reflected at multiple different angles, which is called scattering. Though paper may look smooth to the eye, it really is rough, as can be seen through a microscope; therefore, light *does* scatter when it strikes paper, which does *not* stop scattering (D). The scattering of light does not prevent us from reading at any angle (C), but actually enables us to read print or writing on paper from any angle because its rough surface reflects light waves in all directions.

92. C: The amount that a transparent medium slows down the speed of light through it is called the refraction index. The normal line (A) is an imaginary line that runs at a right angle to the surface of a medium; in the example given, it would be the waterline in the glass of water. The wavelength (B) of the light becomes shorter in proportion to how much the speed of light is slowed by the medium (but the medium does not change the frequency of the light wave, which is a property of the light source). The angle of refraction (D) is the degree to which the light wave is bent by the medium. As an example of refraction indices, diamonds trap light and slow its speed more than water because they are much denser and harder than water; thus, they sparkle more than water does and have a higher refraction index than water.

93. A: The reason the sky looks blue to us is because the earth's atmosphere absorbs the wavelengths of all colors of light in the spectrum except for the wavelengths of the color blue, which it reflects back so that we see it. Therefore (B) is incorrect. Glass appears transparent to us; however, it is really only transparent to the light frequencies (wavelengths) that we can see, but to ultraviolet light frequencies, which we cannot see, glass is actually opaque. Wood, metal, and other materials look opaque to us *not* because they reflect light (D), but rather because they absorb light.

94. B: Heat is transferred three ways: radiation, convection, and conduction. In radiation (A), no medium (matter) or contact is required. Radiation can pass through empty space, as in electromagnetic or infrared radiation. Heat from the sun and from lightbulbs are radiation. In convection, continuous currents circulate as warmer parts of gas or liquid rise to cooler areas, and cooler ones take their place. For example, as the surface of the earth warms, the air above it warms, the warm air rises, and cooler air takes its place. Convection currents are also evident in water when we boil it. In conduction (C), direct contact of matter is required. When one substance is heated, its molecules increase their vibration, striking adjacent molecules and transferring energy to them. This moves energy from the hotter part of the substance to its cooler part. Highly conductive materials, like metal, transfer heat faster. Since (B) is correct, (D) is incorrect.

95. D: The planet Earth is actually a giant magnet; this is why compasses, which contain magnets, always point north. All magnets have two poles; one is north or north-seeking and the other is south or south-seeking. The opposite poles of magnets attract rather than repel one another (A). The like poles of magnets repel rather than attract one another (B). Magnets need not touch to attract or repel each other (C); they can do this from distances as well. The effective range of a magnet to attract or repel is known as its magnetic field.

96. A: Newton's First Law of Motion states that an object at rest tends to stay at rest, and an object in motion tends to stay in motion, unless or until an opposing force changes that. Thus, the rock's sitting on the ground is because an object at rest tends to stay at rest. Newton's Third Law of Motion states that for every action, there is an equal and opposite reaction. This explains the rock's reaction of traveling when you kick it. The rock's traveling for however long it does is because an object in motion tends to stay in motion. Newton's Second Law of Motion states that force equals mass times acceleration ($F = ma$), so moving objects maintain the same speed unless or until some force changes this. The force of friction slows the rock's speed, and the force of the earth's gravity causes the rock to fall back to the ground.

97. B: Vibration is caused by anything physical moving rapidly back and forth. When an object vibrates, the vibrations disturb the medium surrounding it, which may be solid matter, liquids, or gases like the air. Sound does not cause vibrations in the air (A) but vice versa: vibrations are a type of energy. The sound caused by vibration is acoustic energy, and vibratory movements disturb their medium, like the air. Sound causes vibrations not only in the air, but also in the ear (C) when they reach it. Whereas sound waves traveling through the air and through the outer and middle ear are acoustic energy, once they reach the inner ear, it converts that acoustic energy into electrical energy that is sent via nerves to the brain (D).

98. B: Neptune is the farthest of the planets listed from the sun. Mercury (A) is the closest planet in our solar system from the sun. In increasing order of distance from the sun, Venus is second; Earth is third; Mars is fourth; Jupiter (C) is fifth; and Saturn (D) is sixth. Since Pluto was demoted from the status of planet to dwarf planet in 2006 when technology advances permitted clearer observation of it, it is no longer considered the farthest planet from the sun as it is no longer considered a planet. This makes Neptune the farthest planet away from the sun.

99. B: Erosion is the natural process of weather wearing down landforms on the surface of the Earth. It does not cause natural matter like rocks, dirt, and sand to disappear (A); rather, it causes them to change in form and location. Erosion can consist of both mechanical processes, e.g., the breaking into pieces of rock, and also chemical processes (C), e.g., the dissolution of rock in water. Erosion both breaks down some areas of the land and builds up others (D) by transporting eroded

sediment elsewhere. For example, rivers break down the material of mountains and carry the broken-down sediment downstream, where it accumulates at the mouths of rivers and creates new landforms like deltas and swamps.

100. B: Sedimentary rocks are formed in layers on the surface of the Earth when the results of erosion and other processes deposit sediment. Some sedimentary rock remains loose; some is cemented together by chemicals, minerals, or electrical attraction. Igneous rock (C) is formed when volcanoes erupt, spewing lava onto the Earth's surface where it cools and hardens into rock. Metamorphic rock is formed when igneous and sedimentary rocks deeply buried in the crust of the Earth are subjected to extreme heat and/or pressure. These forces change, i.e., metamorphose, the structure of the rocks, creating metamorphic rock. Therefore, (D) is incorrect.

101. B: Certain primitive insects, including dragonflies, grasshoppers, and cockroaches, undergo an incomplete metamorphosis in their life cycle. A metamorphosis is a change in form. In insects, a complete metamorphosis, as butterflies (A) undergo, includes the stages of egg, larva, pupa (called a chrysalis in butterflies), and imago, the adult form. An incomplete metamorphosis in insects includes an egg, larval, and adult stage, but no pupa. Amphibians (C), like frogs, toads, and newts, undergo complete metamorphoses. For example, frogs go from eggs to tadpoles living underwater and breathing with gills to adults living on land and breathing with lungs, also spending part of the time in the water and laying its eggs there. In general, a complete metamorphosis features clearly distinct stages of development, whereas an incomplete metamorphosis features more gradual changes. Birds, fish, spiders, and mammals (D) including humans have simple life cycles with no metamorphoses.

102. C: The relationship between termites and bacteria in their digestive systems is mutualistic, meaning both organisms benefit. Termites live on wood, but their digestive systems cannot break down cellulose in wood. Bacteria in their digestive tracts do this for them. Termites benefit from the nourishment; bacteria in return benefit from a place to live and nourishment from the termites. In parasitic (A) relationships, one organism benefits but the other is harmed. An example is tapeworms in animal digestive tracts: tapeworms benefit from the food eaten by their hosts, but hosts are deprived of nourishment and suffer tissue damage. Ecological (B) relationships are any regular interactions between different organisms that benefit one or both. In commensalistic (D) relationships, one organism benefits and the other does not but is unharmed. An example is barnacles on whales. Water currents created as whales swim deliver food to barnacles. Whales get no benefit from barnacles, but are unhurt by them.

Health and Physical Education

103. A: The American Recovery and Reinvestment Act, among other provisions, allotted funds to prevent chronic disease as a way to promote wellness. This initiative targets obesity and tobacco use as the two most preventable causes of disability and death in America today. Alcohol use {(B), (C)} and the abuse of alcohol and other drugs (D) are not considered as prevalent or as preventable as obesity and the use of tobacco.

104. D: Carefully choosing which fish to eat (A) can avoid or limit toxicity from mercury ingested by the fish. Smaller fish generally contain less mercury than larger ones, and different types of fish and the locations where they lived also affect their mercury levels. Preparing infant formula and cooking foods in cold water (B) can prevent toxicity from lead in water pipes, which hot water dissolves more readily than cold water. Protecting children from exposure to paint in older houses

(C) also protects them from lead poisoning because in the past, most interior home paints were lead-based. Today, newer paint manufacturing uses safer, nontoxic, or less toxic ingredients, though parents should still make sure whether paint contains lead or not.

105. C: The aorta originates at the heart and is the largest artery in the human body. There is not one atrium (A) but two atria, which are chambers of the heart along with the two ventricles. The pulmonary (B) artery carries blood from the heart to the lungs to be oxygenated (the term pulmonary refers to the lungs). There is not one vena cava (D) but two, the superior and inferior vena cavae, which are blood vessels that empty blood into the right atrium of the heart.

106. D: Joints are the junctions of bones, i.e., the places where bones connect or meet with each other. Ligaments (A) are bands of fibrous connective tissue that connect the bones, forming joints. Tendons (B) are elastic connective tissues that connect the muscles to the bones. Cartilage (C) is fibrous connective tissue that covers the surfaces of bones to keep them from rubbing against and damaging one another.

107. D: The human central nervous system includes the autonomic nervous system, which works without our conscious control, and the voluntary nervous system, which we can control. The sympathetic and parasympathetic nervous systems are both divisions of the autonomic nervous system. Neither of them is part of the voluntary nervous system {(B), (C)}. The sympathetic nervous system, not the parasympathetic, stimulates the heartbeat as well as perspiration and vasoconstriction (the contraction of blood vessels), whereas the parasympathetic nervous system, not the sympathetic (A), stimulates the muscular movements of the organs, as well as the secretions of the glands.

108. A: Parts of the large intestine include the cecum, colon, rectum, and anus. The colon itself includes sections called the ascending colon, transverse colon, sigmoid colon, and descending colon. The ileum (B), jejunum (C), and duodenum (D) are all parts of the small intestine rather than the large intestine. The small intestine performs most of the digestive system's digestion and absorption; the large intestine completes the digestion and absorption processes and transports wastes for elimination.

109. D: The human pancreas is both an endocrine gland and an exocrine gland. Endocrine glands secrete internally, directly into the bloodstream and lymphatic system without using ducts. Exocrine glands secrete externally to other body parts through ducts. The pancreas works as an endocrine gland by secreting the hormone insulin to control the metabolism of sugars. It works as an exocrine gland by secreting digestive juice into the duodenum to support digestion. Therefore the pancreas is not only an exocrine gland (A) or only an endocrine gland (B) but both, so that it is neither one (C) is incorrect.

110. D: Malnutrition is not only caused by eating too little; it is also caused by eating foods that are not nutritious, eating unbalanced diets, and not getting enough of all necessary nutrients. Thus, people can eat too much and become overweight, but if most of the calories they consume are "empty", i.e., they contain few or no vitamins, minerals, protein, healthy fats, or fiber, they can suffer malnutrition. In fact, overconsumption of refined carbohydrates that lack fiber instead of whole grains; saturated and trans fats instead of monounsaturated and polyunsaturated fats; and processed foods instead of fruits and vegetables contribute to both obesity and malnutrition. Anxiety, depression, and other emotional factors can not only disrupt sleeping and eating, but also

cause high blood pressure and heart disease (A). Stress and family dysfunction can cause both emotional and physical illness (B). Air pollution is found both to aggravate and to cause asthma (C).

111. C: Iron deficiencies in children have been found to cause symptoms of shortened attention spans, attentional deficits, and irritability similar to the symptoms of Attention Deficit/Hyperactivity Disorder (ADHD), as well as fatigue. Children who skip breakfast (A) have been found to perform with lower speed and accuracy than normal on problem-solving measures. Children who regularly miss meals (B) in general (not just breakfast) have been found to get sick more often and be absent from school more. Children with protein deficiencies (D) are found to have lower achievement test scores than peers getting enough protein.

112. C: Babies typically can play "pattycake" between 7–15 months of age, at an average age of around 9 months. They typically can pull up to stand between 5–12 months, at an average age of around 8 months. They typically develop the pincer grasp (D) for picking up small objects between 6–12 months. Children with normal development typically can jump in place (C) between 17–30 months of age, at an average age of around 23½ months, i.e., almost two years old.

113. B: Children's motor skills develop most rapidly from 2–6 years. Between these ages, children typically learn to walk, run, skip, hop, gallop, jump, skip, and climb, using the large muscles; gross-motor eye-hand coordination to throw and catch balls; and eye-hand coordination with fine-motor skills for tasks of manipulating small objects like using eating utensils, drawing and writing, fastening and undoing buttons and zippers, etc. From birth to 2 years (A), first children's sensory abilities develop. Their motor skill developments during these ages include rolling over, sitting up, crawling, pulling up, standing alone, walking, assisted stair-climbing, and jumping in place among gross motor skills, and playing pattycake, stacking two blocks, scribbling, and picking up small things among fine motor skills. However, their motor development is faster after age 2 than before. Children's gross and fine motor skills become more complex and refined from 6–8 years (C), but development is not as fast as before age 6, as many basic skills have already developed. Since (B) is correct, (D) is incorrect.

114. A: The Babinski reflex occurs when the sole of the foot is firmly stroked vertically: the big toe moves upward and the other toes fan outward. This is normal in newborns and disappears anytime between 1 and 2 years of age. The stepping reflex (B), wherein newborns automatically perform a stepping motion when held upright with their feet on or near a surface, typically disappears around the age of 2 months. The palmar grasping reflex (C), wherein a baby will grasp an offered adult finger in his or her fist, typically disappears around 3–4 months. The tonic reflex (D), wherein newborns assume the "fencing position" with the head turned to one side, one arm in front of the eyes and the other arm bent at the elbow, typically disappears around the age of 4 months.

115. B: Cephalocaudal means from head to toe, and proximodistal means from near to far, not vice versa (A). An example of proximodistal development is that infants develop control of their arms before control of their fingers (B) because their arms are closer to the center than their fingers are. An example of cephalocaudal development is that babies develop control of their heads before control of their legs, not vice versa (D) because development proceeds from the head downward. Cephalocaudal and proximodistal development are the same before and after birth, rather than differing (C).

116. A: Through engaging in physical activity, children learn to expend physical and mental effort and to persevere when they encounter difficulty. These experiences not only enhance their self-esteem, i.e., feeling and thinking well of themselves, but also their self-efficacy, i.e., their feeling that

they are competent to perform specific tasks. Children's motor skills typically develop younger than their language skills, not vice versa (B); hence physical activity is an important way for them to express themselves before they can do so verbally. Children not only develop their motor skills through participating in physical games and sports; they also learn social skills (C) from interacting with peers and adults during these activities. Children not only enjoy the social interaction; normally, young children naturally seek out physical activity (D) and get pleasure from physical movement.

117. B: According to research by the Institute of Medicine (2013), more physically active children can focus their attention better than children who are less active (A). Children who get more exercise show better performance on standardized academic tests (B). More physical activity also improves children's working memory (C) and their problem-solving skills (D).

Creative and Performing Arts

118. B: If the class unit is on space travel, then an art activity of constructing models of rocket ships would integrate art thematically into the curriculum more than painting portraits of classmates (A), exploring different art materials all in one color (C), or using art work to express their feelings (D) would. Assigning art projects focused on the same themes that are central to their curriculum units and/or lessons is one way that teachers can integrate art across academic content areas.

119. C: Japanese bowls made for the traditional tea ceremony is an example of art that serves a physical purpose. Photography by Dorothea Lange, Gordon Parks, Arthur Rothstein, Walker Evans, and others, commissioned by the Farm Security Administration (FSA) during the Great Depression, showed the extreme poverty, hunger, and suffering of many people; this is an example of art that serves a social purpose. Da Vinci's "Last Supper" (B) painting, like many other artworks with religious themes, is an example of art that serves a personal purpose. Satire in art, like some of Goya's works (D), is an example of art that serves a social purpose.

120. A: In the process of creating art, the artist first imagines what ideas and feelings s/he wants to express. Then s/he plans how to do this by researching, experimenting with, and designing the materials and forms to use and how to work with them to accomplish the results desired. The artist then creates an artistic product, evaluates how effective it is and how satisfied s/he is with it, and refines the product based on the evaluation. Once the artist is satisfied with the product, s/he then presents it to an audience of others who can participate with and respond to it.

121. D: Form in visual art represents the three-dimensional projection of shape. It has dimension and volume; in three-dimensional artworks like sculptures, form has actual mass. In two-dimensional artworks like drawings and paintings, form does not have real mass; however, it can appear to have mass through the artist's visual techniques. Shapes in art may be positive, i.e., defined by outlines; or negative, i.e., defined only by the edges of surrounding shapes (A). Biomorphic shapes are shapes seen in nature. While some shapes found in nature can be geometric, like circles, ovals, and stars (e.g., starfish), many biomorphic shapes are not perfectly geometric or geometric at all (B). Value in visual art is not dependent on color (C); value means the range of lights and darks in the artwork, no matter what colors are or are not used.

122. B: Green is a secondary color because it is produced by mixing the two primary colors blue and yellow. Yellow (A), blue (C), and red (D) are the only primary colors. Green, orange, and purple are

the secondary colors. Orange is made by mixing red and yellow. Purple is made by mixing blue and red.

123. B: Complementary colors are found opposite or across from each other on the color wheel. Complementary colors are not adjacent or next to one another on the color wheel (A); colors next to each other on the color wheel are called analogous colors, e.g., blue and green; green and yellow; yellow and orange; orange and red. When two complementary colors are mixed in equal parts, they create brown, not black (C). When one color is cool, its complementary color is warm and vice versa, rather than both of them being either warm or cool (D). For example, blue and orange are complementary; yellow and purple are complementary; and red and green are complementary. These colors complement each other, i.e., they go well together: they balance each other by being opposites. If you stare at one bright color (like red) long enough and then look at a blank white surface, you will see the complementary color (like green).

124. A: The pitch of an individual note in music is determined by the frequency of the individual sound wave that produces that note. High-frequency sound waves produce high-pitched notes, middle frequencies produce medium-pitched notes, and low-frequency sound waves produce low-pitched notes. Particular frequencies equate to specific notes that have been assigned letter names in modern music, from A through G, with sharps and flats representing half-steps between notes. Tempo (B) is the relative speed at which music is played. Rhythm (C) includes time signature, i.e., the number of beats per measure; patterns among longer (held for more beats) and shorter (held for fewer beats) notes; and how notes are produced, like smoothly connected or *legato* vs. sharply disconnected or *staccato*. Harmony (D) is the combination of more than one note or pitch sounded at the same time, producing a pleasing effect. Two-part harmonies are commonly named by their intervals, e.g., thirds, fourths, fifths, sixths, etc. Harmonies with more than two parts are called chords.

125. C: Texture is something we commonly think of as tactile, i.e., what we can feel with our hands or on our skin. However, in visual art, texture can be seen as well as felt; hence texture can exist in two-dimensional art like drawings and paintings as well as in three-dimensional art like sculptures (A). Texture refers not only to roughness or smoothness, but also to wetness or dryness (B), softness or hardness, etc. In some paintings and other two-dimensional art, texture can be actually felt, as when sandpaper or other rough surfaces are used in places or paint is built up to create a palpable texture; or it can be seen rather than felt, as when something is drawn or painted to look bumpy or glassy, etc. (D).

126. B: Balance refers to the distribution of visual weight in an artwork. Balance can be symmetrical (A), with equal distribution, or asymmetrical, with unequal and/or unevenly distributed shapes and spaces, yet achieving overall equilibrium. Asymmetrical balance can suggest movement and create tension, which produces psychological balance rather than physical balance (C). Radial balance does involve a central point (D): images radiate from a positive or negative center, in a linear way like the spokes of a wheel or in a circular way like ripples around a pebble dropped into a pond or the growth rings seen in a cut tree.

Practice Test #2

Practice Questions

Language and Literacy

1. Phonological awareness prominently features knowing the _____ in one's native language.
   a. Sounds
   b. Letters
   c. Words
   d. Spelling

2. A young child whose phonological awareness skills are developing well can typically:
   a. Think about phonemes.
   b. Talk about phonemes.
   c. Manipulate phonemes.
   d. Do all of these things.

3. Which is true of young children with typical development in phonological awareness skills?
   a. They can recognize rhyming words, but not produce them.
   b. They can segment speech sounds, but cannot blend them.
   c. They can change words by substituting different phonemes.
   d. They can add, but not remove, phonemes to change words.

4. Which of the following is correct regarding the benefits of direct instruction in phonological and phonemic awareness (PPA) for young children?
   a. Preschool-aged children benefit from PPA instruction, but first-grade students do not.
   b. Preschool children with delays in language development benefit from PPA instruction.
   c. Preschool-aged children with articulation disorders are not helped by PPA instruction.
   d. School-aged children with spelling disorders reap no benefits from instruction in PPA.

5. Which of the following terms corresponds most closely to the definition of establishing the Alphabetic Principle and teaching word-decoding and -encoding skills?
   a. Phonics
   b. Phonemic awareness
   c. Phonological awareness
   d. These all fit the definition

6. A child who understands that the word *books* means two or more while *book* means one is demonstrating an understanding of:
   a. Phonology
   b. Morphology
   c. Syntax
   d. Semantics

7. Which of the following is NOT an EC teacher practice recommended by experts to support language development?
    a. Describing the children's activities aloud using words to model verbalizing actions
    b. Repeating what each child says and then adding some additional information to it
    c. Supplying the majority of speech in the classroom to provide a model for children
    d. Commenting on and describing properties of concrete objects children are using

8. Students learning English as a second language (ESL) are typically found to reach the Advanced Fluency stage of speaking English within roughly what time frame?
    a. Within approximately the first six months of learning
    b. Within approximately the first one to three years of learning
    c. Within approximately the first three to five years of learning
    d. Within approximately the first five to seven years of learning

9. Disorders of speech rate and rhythm are most associated with:
    a. Stuttering
    b. Cleft palate
    c. Jargon aphasia
    d. Motor apraxia

10. Which of the following is the LEAST likely etiology for delayed language development in childhood?
    a. Mental retardation
    b. Neurological damage
    c. Environmental deprivation
    d. Low levels of self-esteem

11. To learn the sounds spelled by printed/written letters and recognize printed words, children must:
    a. Know the order of the alphabet.
    b. Know the names of the letters.
    c. Know how to write the letters.
    d. Know letter shapes, not names.

12. To strengthen beginning preschoolers' alphabetic knowledge, teachers should:
    a. Focus on cumulative reviews of letter-sound matches children have learned.
    b. Focus on creating occasions for children to practice new letter-sound matches.
    c. Balance knowledge reviews with learning practice, including phonetic spellings.
    d. Avoid supplying children with incorrect phonetic spellings of words they know.

13. Which is correct for teachers to consider when teaching ESL/ELL students English?
    a. Spanish-speaking children learn to sound out words in the same ways as in English.
    b. The less English (L2) proficiency students have, the more they rely on cues from L1.
    c. ELL students use the same amount of cognitive energy as native English speakers.
    d. The concept of directionality in reading and writing is the same across all languages.

14. Print awareness skills typically demonstrated independently by preschoolers include:
    a. Recognizing printed letters, but not necessarily also printed words.
    b. Reciting the alphabet, but not identifying single letters in isolation.
    c. Recognizing printed words, but not using these for communicating.
    d. Reciting ABCs; recognizing letters and words; print communication.

15. Which of these is true of how the instructional strategy of Expanded Book Reading enhances literacy development and reading comprehension?
    a. Teachers should avoid summarizing books in advance for students.
    b. Teachers should not have children predict a book's possible content.
    c. Teachers can informally assess comprehension via student retelling.
    d. Teachers cannot use this strategy with literacy across the curriculum.

16. Which of the following is accurate regarding the 3N instructional strategy for EC literacy development?
    a. The Notice step involves having the student observe his or her own literacy strategies.
    b. The Nudge step involves teachers' providing scaffolding to raise student literacy levels.
    c. The Narrate step involves having the student verbally describe his/her literacy activity.
    d. The Narrate step involves having the student verbally reflect on the literacy activity.

17. Which of these is a strategy most applicable to evaluating a young student's reading comprehension of narrative writing?
    a. Whether the student can retell a story that s/he has just read
    b. Whether the student can decode unfamiliar words in the story
    c. Whether the student can invent spellings for unfamiliar words
    d. Whether the student can identify and produce rhyming words

18. What is true about children's books that educators term "predictable books"?
    a. These are books that feature unoriginal plots.
    b. They enable immediate participation and practice.
    c. These are books not incorporating imagination.
    d. They are not naturally appealing to young children.

19. Which of the following children's book is the best example of the modern fantasy genre?
    a. *Old Possum's Book of Practical Cats* by T.S. Eliot
    b. The *Fables* by Aesop
    c. *Winnie the Pooh* by A. A. Milne
    d. *Lincoln: A Photobiography* by Russell Freedman

20. Which of the following is an example of EC student difficulty with word decoding and phonics?
    a. A child matches up the letters s/he sees with corresponding sounds.
    b. A child matches up the sounds s/he hears with corresponding letters.
    c. A child includes letter sounds s/he has learned in his/her written work.
    d. A child looks at the first one or two letters of a word to guess what it is.

21. Which of the following activities requires ESL students to use conversational English rather than academic English?
    a. Understanding their school textbooks
    b. Solving mathematical word problems
    c. Understanding a teacher's questions
    d. Dealing with new/abstract concepts

22. Which of these is accurate regarding a word wall for building young children's vocabularies?
    a. A word wall contains only words and no pictures.
    b. A word wall includes synonyms for target words.
    c. A word wall only has pictures for guessing words.
    d. A word wall focuses on target words, not others.

23. Which of these is correct regarding children's reading fluency?
    a. Sounding choppy when reading out loud indicates a lack of fluency.
    b. Fluency is only an issue for children when they are reading out loud.
    c. Reading aloud without expression is no issue as long as it is accurate.
    d. Reading fluency is measured by reading speed, but not by accuracy.

24. Which statement is most accurate regarding young students' reading comprehension?
    a. Students missing main ideas while noticing details more likely have comprehension issues.
    b. Missing either the main ideas or the details of the text signifies comprehension problems.
    c. Students who cannot repeat any details but get the main idea have good comprehension.
    d. If a student gets the main ideas, the ability to retell logical event sequences is immaterial.

25. Of the following, which is accurate regarding signs that a student might have dyslexia?
    a. Children with dyslexia tend to miss entire words in reading, but not syllables in words.
    b. Dyslexic children often misspell words, but will rarely confuse similar-sounding words.
    c. Dyslexics with good fine-motor and word-processing skills often still handwrite poorly.
    d. Children with dyslexia typically are willing to read aloud despite their numerous errors.

26. In which of the following stages of spelling development do children use letters to represent speech sounds in a systematic and understandable way?
    a. Correct
    b. Transitional
    c. Semiphonetic
    d. Phonetic

27. Conclusions of linguistic researchers into children's invented spellings are best described thus:
    a. Spelling is primarily a process of simply memorizing the words.
    b. Spelling is simply a process of letter-to-sound correspondence.
    c. Spelling is a developmental process informing comprehension.
    d. Spellings children invent vary widely across diverse individuals.

28. In which of five identified stages of children's writing development do they typically learn to write vowels, initial and final sounds/letters of words, and experiment with sentence construction and punctuation?
   a. Conventional writing and spelling
   b. Letters and spaces
   c. Letter-like forms and shapes
   d. Letters

29. Which of the following statements is correct about findings regarding the role of writing in learning?
   a. Improving students' reading skills and their writing skills reciprocally reinforce one another.
   b. Normally developing students are found to be able to learn to write well without teaching.
   c. Improving students' writing skills is not found to have any effect on their learning capacity.
   d. Student writing skills improve when their reading skills improve, but the reverse is not true.

30. In which step of the POWER writing instruction strategy should the teacher help the student to see whether s/he has grouped similar ideas together?
   a. The Organization step
   b. The Planning step
   c. The Writing step
   d. The Editing step

31. In the language levels of a child's early writing efforts, writing letters develops before writing words. Of the following, which is typically the *latest* in the developmental sequence of writing?
   a. Phrases
   b. Sentences
   c. Paragraphs
   d. Punctuation

32. A traditional habit of teachers, when evaluating student writing, has been to:
   a. Focus on how well the student's writing functions to convey meaning.
   b. Focus on how effective the student's writing is to fulfill its purpose(s).
   c. Focus on a combination of the form and function of student writing.
   d. Focus on writing's appearance and form more than its functionality.

33. If a student writes "washington dc," this is an example of which kind of error?
   a. Grammatical
   b. Punctuation
   c. Capitalization
   d. Both B and C

34. Which of the following is NOT an example of problems or errors in student handwriting?
   a. Faulty alignment
   b. Incorrect spacing
   c. Dangling participle
   d. Writing is illegible

35. Concerning motivating young children to engage in writing activities, which is true?
    a. Children should learn to write their own critiques of authors/books before evaluating them.
    b. Children are motivated to write up classmate interviews by teacher modeling and guidance.
    c. Teachers should never deliberately commit errors when transcribing the children's dictation.
    d. Teachers can bring in samples of their own writing, but asking children to do so will backfire.

36. When applying the following identified motivational factors specifically to student motivation to write, which one applies more to overall writing skills than to specific writing tasks?
    a. Students' beliefs about their self-efficacy
    b. Students' goals for performance/mastery
    c. Students' interest/value for writing tasks
    d. Students' attributions for failure/success

Mathematics

37. Regarding problem-solving skills and how they apply to mathematics, which of the following is true?
    a. In math, there is always only one possible right answer to a given question.
    b. Students must learn the concept that multiple solutions to a problem exist.
    c. Problem-solving skills are important for only certain parts of mathematics.
    d. Problem-solving skills can be learned equally well with or without practice.

38. Of the following examples of preschooler behaviors, which one is developmentally normal and typical, but less an example of using mathematical concepts than the others?
    a. A child collects three of his toys, looks at them, and says, "I have three toys here."
    b. A child sees three toys, holds up three fingers, and says, "This is how many toys."
    c. A child with two cookies says, "If you give me one more cookie, I will have three."
    d. A child with two cookie halves says, "I have more than" a child with a whole cookie.

39. Which of these is the most valid advice for adults in playing mental math games with young children?
    a. It is important for the adult and child to take turns posing and solving story problems.
    b. It is more important for the adult to give the child correct answers than ask questions.
    c. It is more important for the game to be strictly factual, like most math tests, than fun.
    d. It is important to give children unknown variable or number games in early childhood.

40. Very young children naturally think about mathematical concepts in ways that are primarily:
    a. Formal.
    b. Logical.
    c. Intuitive.
    d. Deductive.

41. Which of the following teacher practices can help children learn to apply the math they learn in school to everyday problem solving in real life?
    a. Emphasize the view of mathematics as a discipline composed of rules and procedures.
    b. Work to form connections between children's intuitive math thinking and formal math.
    c. Avoid introducing concrete objects to manipulate when teaching formal mathematics.
    d. Omit real-life examples of math concepts or math vocabulary describing child activities.

42. When an adult pours liquid into containers of different sizes and invites a child to speculate about which container will hold more, this activity applies which of the following mathematical concepts?
   a. Conservation of liquid volume
   b. Measurement
   c. Estimation
   d. All these

43. Which of these examples of symbolic representation and emerging math skills in children typically develops at the *latest* (oldest) ages?
   a. Drawing pictures and maps
   b. Counting using their fingers
   c. Making graphs to show data
   d. Making tallies using tick-marks

44. If a child in a preschool learning center likes to sort rocks by their colors, which of the following teacher practices best represents an emphasis on building the child's problem-solving skills?
   a. The teacher asks afterward how else s/he could sort them.
   b. The teacher tells the child that s/he is classifying the rocks.
   c. The teacher asks the child which way s/he is sorting rocks.
   d. These all equally represent building problem-solving skills.

45. In addition to math, in which other area(s) of life do we most tend to see and/or create patterns and relationships?
   a. Works of art
   b. Pieces of music
   c. Articles of clothing
   d. In all of these areas

46. Which statement is true regarding children's basic understanding of patterns and relationships?
   a. This understanding is unrelated to children's understanding of repetition.
   b. Having this is unlikely to inform children in any understanding of rhythm.
   c. Children can understand grouping things into categories if they have this.
   d. Children need different knowledge for ordering things by size or degree.

47. Which of the following activities is most focused on children's *identifying* patterns?
   a. Stringing beads with different colors in a certain order to make a necklace design
   b. Counting the number of blue dots before a green dot appears in a printed fabric
   c. Arranging alternating pieces of different sizes and gluing them to paper or board
   d. Hopping two times on one foot, then the other; then three times each; four; etc.

48. Which is most accurate regarding what constitutes number sense in young children?
   a. Number sense encompasses understanding of all the ways that we apply numbers.
   b. Number sense is understanding that we use numbers to communicate information.
   c. Number sense is understanding that we use numbers for manipulating information.
   d. Number sense is knowing we use numbers to describe quantities and relationships.

49. What statement is true about helping young children to develop number sense and other numeracy skills?
    a. These skills are promoted when adults and children count, sort, and discuss numbers together.
    b. When helping young children, adults should neither use nor encourage counting on the fingers.
    c. When counting multiple objects, both adults and children should avoid pointing to each object.
    d. Adults should not correct young children when they repeat or skip numbers while they count.

50. To help young children learn geometry, which of these should adults do *first?*
    a. Ask them to name various shapes, angles, and three-dimensional figures on sight
    b. Tell them the names for different shapes, three-dimensional figures, and angles
    c. Ask young children to trace drawings of different shapes and figures with fingers
    d. Invite young children to make drawings of different shapes and figures on paper

51. Which of these is the best example of a hands-on activity that will help young children learn geometry concepts?
    a. Giving children differently sized and shaped boxes and having them draw pictures of these
    b. Giving children drawings of differently sized and shaped objects to match with real objects
    c. Giving children big boxes and furniture to go into/out of, over/under, around/through, etc.
    d. Giving children boxes and furniture and simple disposable cameras for photographing them

52. What is true about facilitating young children's early development of measurement skills?
    a. Adults should discourage children from using their own personal measuring units.
    b. Adults should teach children standardized measurement units in isolated lessons.
    c. Adults should explain measuring to children when demonstrating everyday tasks.
    d. Adults should ask children to participate in everyday tasks and discuss measuring.

53. A young child in Piaget's Preoperational stage of cognitive development is most likely to draw which of the following conclusions?
    a. That one whole cookie and another cookie the same size cut into four pieces are the same amount
    b. That one whole cookie is a larger amount than another cookie the same size cut up into four pieces
    c. That one whole cookie is the same amount as one piece of the same size cookie cut into four pieces
    d. That one whole cookie is not as much as another cookie the same size that is cut up into four pieces

54. Which of the following is the best example of an activity to help young children gain an informal understanding of fractions?
    a. Adults giving children slices of pizza and having them compare the slice sizes
    b. Adults asking young children to divide beads into piles equaling 1/6, 2/6, 3/6
    c. Adults asking children to help cut a pan of brownies into pieces of equal sizes
    d. Adults giving children whole apples and halved apples, asking which is bigger

55. What is true about helping young children to learn how to estimate quantities?
   a. Adults should avoid using vocabulary terms of approximation in everyday conversations.
   b. Adults should ask children to guess quantities, and then test these using measurements.
   c. Adults should always use standardized measurements to describe quantities to children.
   d. Adults should have children practice estimating numbers until they attain precise results.

56. Which of the following would be most useful to help the youngest children understand how to organize information?
   a. A calendar showing children's daily and/or weekly activity plans
   b. A statistical table showing different group rates of achievement
   c. A line graph showing daily or weekly differences in attendance
   d. A weather forecast showing the chances it will snow that week

57. Of the following activities, which is the best example of one that would give preschoolers practice with collecting, organizing, and displaying data?
   a. Having each child choose a favorite color sticker and putting stickers on a chart divided by color
   b. Having each child differentiate solid, 3-D shapes with three sides, four sides, or no sides (round)
   c. Having each child choose a favorite color of sticker and guess the numbers of each color chosen
   d. Having each child receive a sticker for arriving on time with a reward for every five stickers in a row

58. A teacher asks children to sort various objects. First the teacher has them put big things in one box and little things in another box. Then the teacher has the children separate hard things from soft things, etc. Which mathematical concept is most supported by this activity?
   a. Patterning
   b. Classifying
   c. Counting
   d. Ordering

59. For which of the following activities would preschool children most need some understanding of and familiarity with relationships and patterns?
   a. Determining which group has more objects
   b. Comparing 3-D object shapes with 2-D ones
   c. Classifying various objects into sets by color
   d. Matching written numbers with their values

60. Of the following statements, which is true of how children's mathematical counting skills develop?
   a. Learning to count from one to twelve involves more unusual rules.
   b. Learning to count from thirteen to nineteen requires more memorizing.
   c. Learning to count above twenty involves less consistent rules.
   d. Learning to count from twenty to one hundred, children discover base ten.

61. An adult holds a bag filled with variously shaped forms and tells young children to take turns closing their eyes, reaching into the bag, and finding a specified shape like a triangle solely by touch. This activity, which young children enjoy, engages which level(s) of shape perception?
    a. Appearance and naming
    b. Appearance and analysis
    c. Analysis of shapes only
    d. Analysis and naming

62. Most experts in math education find which of the following to be most true about integrating math into all of young children's daily activities in preschool/school?
    a. Taking advantage of "teachable moments"
    b. Applying planned curriculum approaches
    c. Both curricular and natural opportunities
    d. *Systematically* using "teachable moments"

63. Of the following, which is LEAST characteristic of young children's cognitive development as they learn basic mathematical concepts through their everyday activities?
    a. Exploring their environments
    b. Performing mental operations
    c. Manipulating concrete objects
    d. Observing relationships in life

64. Which choice best reflects the skills whose development is supported by young children's developing spatial awareness?
    a. Gross motor skills, coordination, and social skills
    b. Coordination, gross motor skills, fine motor skills
    c. Gross motor skills, fine motor skills, social skills
    d. Coordination, fine motor skills, and social skills

65. When a preschool child solves a simplified jigsaw puzzle with large wood pieces, s/he is demonstrating which early math skill the most?
    a. Making measurements
    b. Part-to-whole relations
    c. Skill for analyzing data
    d. Recognizing patterns

66. Which of the following statements includes a use of a nominal number?
    a. "I was second in line."
    b. "We have seven kids."
    c. "My zip code is 12346."
    d. "Pi equals 3.141592...."

Social Studies

67. An adult places a sticker on a small child's face and then introduces a mirror. When the child sees the sticker in the mirror, s/he reaches toward her/his face to remove it rather than toward the mirror. Which level of self-awareness does this demonstrate?
    a. Permanence
    b. Differentiation
    c. Situation
    d. Identification

68. A typically developing child is shown a TV with live video of herself, and also shown adult researchers who are imitating the child's behaviors. The child can tell the difference between the video and the imitators. This child is most likely:
    a. A newborn
    b. Two years old
    c. Four to seven months
    d. Four to six months

69. Which of the following behaviors typically develops earliest in babies/toddlers/young children?
    a. Coordinating their peer-play behaviors
    b. Sharing toy/object activities with peers
    c. Prosocial, helping, and caring behaviors
    d. Creating "make-believe" play scenarios

70. In a popular set of six conflict-mediation/resolution steps for young children, the first step is to approach the conflict calmly, interrupting any hurtful behaviors; the second step is to acknowledge the children's feelings. Of the subsequent four steps, while comes first?
    a. Gather enough information about the conflict.
    b. Elicit potential solutions; help children pick one.
    c. Reiterate/state over again what the problem is.
    d. Provide the children with support as is needed.

71. Of the four parenting styles identified by psychologists, which one is found most likely to result in children who have problems with authority figures, poor school performance, and poor self-regulation?
    a. Authoritarian
    b. Permissive
    c. Authoritative
    d. Uninvolved

72. According to family systems theory, which family system component reflects the family's physical and emotional environment and its emotional quality?
    a. Hierarchy
    b. Boundaries
    c. Climate
    d. Equilibrium

73. Which of the following are more appreciated by individualistic cultures than by collectivist cultures?
    a. Socially and relationally oriented behaviors
    b. Working together for the good of the group
    c. Interdependence rather than independence
    d. Scientific thinking and manipulation of objects

74. Which statement is most accurate about the interactions of American educators with culturally diverse families?
    a. The problems are encountered primarily by culturally diverse families.
    b. The problems are encountered primarily by the American educators.
    c. The problems are encountered equally by the families and educators.
    d. The problems are encountered usually quite minimally by either group.

75. Regarding cultural influences on parental childcare and education preferences, which result is true?
    a. Hispanic families in the U.S. are found to use preschool centers more.
    b. Hispanic families in the U.S. are found to prefer home/family settings.
    c. Caucasian and Hispanic families in the U.S. use center and home care equally.
    d. Caucasian families in the U.S. are likely to prefer family/home settings.

76. Parents of diverse cultures in the U.S. are found by researchers to vary widely in how much they read to their young children. Which factor(s) is/are *most* responsible for this variation?
    a. All of these factors and more
    b. Differing cultural values
    c. Limited time and money
    d. Native and ESL literacy levels

77. Which statement is most accurate regarding how educators in America can work with parents who are immigrants to this country?
    a. Where parents and educators disagree on educational goals, educators must convince these parents to agree with them.
    b. When children have developmental/learning problems, parents may need educators to inform them of available services.
    c. When parents from other cultures do not advocate for their children to get needed services, this is due to a lack of interest.
    d. When immigrant parents do not advocate for their children to get needed services, they are resisting confronting problems.

78. According to research into differences among culturally diverse parents in America's age expectations for EC developmental milestones, which of the following is correct?
    a. Assessment data are no more likely to be misinterpreted when educators and parents have different rather than the same cultures.
    b. Due to cultural variations in when children achieve milestones, educators need not worry about developmental assessments.
    c. What parents from one culture view as developmentally normal can indicate developmental delay to parents from another culture.
    d. Regardless of parental cultural background, not reaching a developmental milestone by a certain age is always a cause for concern.

79. In geography, which of the following is the best example of the concept of area differentiation?
  a. Fishermen find more use in the ocean than farmers; naturalists use forests more than academics.
  b. A region where farming is the main pursuit is rural; one where manufacturing dominates is urban.
  c. Land that is settled first or most frequently is often near natural resources like water, forests, etc.
  d. In one village, the predominant occupation is farming; in another village, fishing is more prevalent.

80. In cartography, which of the following types of map most likely identifies the United States of America, the state of New York, and New York City?
  a. A political map
  b. A physical map
  c. A thematic map
  d. A semantic map

81. Of the following, which pair can *both* create visual pictures of changes in quantities across periods of time that make it easy to see trends, like increases or decreases?
  a. A pie chart and number column
  b. A line graph and a bar graph
  c. A line graph and a pie chart
  d. A bar graph and number column

82. Which statement is correct about criteria for student development of chronological thinking?
  a. Students should be able to interpret data displayed on time lines by high school.
  b. Students should be able to analyze historical duration patterns by middle school.
  c. Students should be able to measure time mathematically by middle school grades.
  d. Students should be able to analyze historical succession patterns by middle school.

83. Of these statements, what is most correct about teaching citizenship to young children?
  a. EC teachers should use factual material rather than fictional children's literature.
  b. Young children are cognitively unable to relate narratives to citizenship concepts.
  c. Discussions of rules are best begun with reading real rules rather than narratives.
  d. Small-group activities having children write and then revise class rules are useful.

Science

84. Which infant/toddler activity is most related to their learning part-to-whole relationships?
  a. Observing that some objects roll away, while others do not
  b. Waking up wet and hungry and then being changed and fed
  c. Crawling or climbing under, into, onto, and around furniture
  d. Building structures out of blocks and then taking them apart

85. What is true about the adult's role in a preschooler's naturalistic, exploratory activities?
    a. Because children spontaneously initiate these activities, adults need not add anything.
    b. Adults should overtly direct children to engage in specific activities chosen by the adult.
    c. Adults should give children's appropriate actions positive reinforcement and feedback.
    d. As children are motivated by curiosity and novelty, adults need not supply any material.

86. In the scientific method, which of the following steps should come first?
    a. Formulating a hypothesis
    b. Asking a research question
    c. Conducting an experiment
    d. Reporting proof or disproof

87. Among the states of matter, water vapor is classified as:
    a. A gas.
    b. A solid.
    c. A liquid.
    d. None of these.

88. The gases argon, helium, krypton, neon, radon, and xenon are known as:
    a. Noble gases.
    b. Unstable gases.
    c. Compound gases.
    d. They are all of these.

89. Which of these statements is true regarding magnetism?
    a. Only certain electric motors have magnets in them.
    b. The planet Earth in itself constitutes a huge magnet.
    c. Compasses but not tape recorders contain magnets.
    d. Generators contain magnets but telephones do not.

90. Magnetic domains are:
    a. Randomly arranged when they are magnetized.
    b. Found to be unrelated to the spinning of electrons.
    c. Groups of molecules that function as magnets.
    d. Elements of a theory that has been discredited.

91. Which is correct about the atomic structure of electrical properties?
    a. Materials whose atoms have strongly bound electrons conduct.
    b. Materials whose atoms have loose electrons insulate electricity.
    c. Materials with free electrons block the conduction of electricity.
    d. Materials whose atoms feature tightly bound electrons insulate.

92. Of the following, which is a valid example of a heat sink?
    a. A particular type of sinkhole in the ground whose contents generate heat
    b. A high-technology kitchen sink with a heated bowl that runs boiling water
    c. A component in a computer that transfers heat away from the processor
    d. A device invented for diving that uses variable heat levels for submersion

93. Where force = F, mass = m, and acceleration = a, a law of physics states that $F = ma$, i.e., force equals mass times acceleration. This rule is:
    a. Newton's First Law of Motion.
    b. Newton's Second Law of Motion.
    c. Newton's Third Law of Motion.
    d. Not one of Isaac Newton's laws.

94. Sound waves are a form of acoustic energy. When we hear sound, this acoustic energy is converted to electrical energy by our:
    a. Inner ears.
    b. Outer ears.
    c. Middle ears.
    d. Brain parts.

95. One complete revolution of the Earth around the Sun equals:
    a. One day.
    b. One year.
    c. One month.
    d. One century.

96. Limestone is one example of which subtype of sedimentary rock?
    a. Clastic
    b. Organic
    c. Chemical
    d. Pegmatite

97. The behaviors of living organisms are changed and shaped by:
    a. Primarily internal stimuli.
    b. Primarily external stimuli.
    c. Preset genetic programs.
    d. Internal and external cues.

98. In insects whose life cycles include an incomplete metamorphosis, which stage of the metamorphosis does not take place?
    a. The egg
    b. The larva
    c. The imago
    d. The pupa

99. When animals and plants reproduce sexually, they produce _____ in their _____ via _____.
    a. gonads; gametes; mitosis
    b. zygotes; gonads; meiosis
    c. gametes; gonads; meiosis
    d. zygotes; gametes; mitosis

100. Of the following ecological relationships, which ones benefit both organisms involved?
   a. Commensalistic relationships
   b. Mutualistic relationships
   c. Parasitic relationships
   d. None of these does

Health and Physical Education

101. The U.S. government's Health and Human Services (HHS) department has enacted a community program focusing on prevention of chronic disease. Which of the following is one of this program's outcome goals?
   a. Decreasing exposure to secondhand smoke
   b. Getting drug dealers off community streets
   c. Increasing tests and diagnoses for diabetes
   d. Banning the sale of certain foods and drinks

102. For adults to protect children from environmental health risk, which of these is true?
   a. House dust that accumulates in homes is not considered a health risk.
   b. Parents should use only cold water to prepare formula to feed babies.
   c. The presence of carbon monoxide gas indoors is normal and harmless.
   d. Infants and young children need sunlight, so it is safe to expose them.

103. Which of these is the largest artery in the human body?
   a. The superior vena cava
   b. The pulmonary artery
   c. The aorta
   d. The heart

104. Which division of the human brain regulates the coordination of motor movements?
   a. The medulla
   b. The midbrain
   c. The cerebrum
   d. The cerebellum

105. Which of the human cranial nerves controls sensation in the face?
   a. The facial nerve (VII)
   b. The vagus nerve (X)
   c. The trigeminal nerve (V)
   d. The hypoglossal nerve (XII)

106. Which part of the human digestive system does the largest amount of digestion and absorption?
   a. The stomach
   b. The small intestine
   c. The large intestine
   d. The descending colon

107. During which age range do children's motor skills normally develop the fastest?
   a. Birth to four years
   b. From one to five years
   c. From three to seven years
   d. From two to six years

108. Which of the following is an example of how emotional/behavioral factors can affect young children's levels of physical activity and fitness?
   a. A child diagnosed with ADHD is physically so overactive that he becomes exhausted.
   b. A child diagnosed with asthma needs monitoring for breathing problems in exercise.
   c. A child diagnosed with diabetes needs exercise watched and coordinated with diet.
   d. A child diagnosed with disabilities needs adaptive equipment for physical activities.

109. What is correct regarding the standards for physical education set forth by the National Association for Sport and Physical Education (NASPE)?
   a. Their criteria for physical fitness do not directly mention health.
   b. They mention social interaction but not self-respect as a benefit.
   c. These standards do not address diet as a part of physical fitness.
   d. They assume exercise confers pleasure and so do not mention it.

110. The World Health Organization recommends that between the ages of five and seventeen, children should do which of the following in terms of physical activity?
   a. At least three weekly sessions of aerobic activity and one hour daily of weight-bearing activity
   b. At least one hour of daily aerobic activity and three weekly sessions of weight-bearing activity
   c. At least three days a week for aerobic activity and three days a week of weight-bearing activity
   d. At least one hour a day for aerobic activity and one hour per day for weight-bearing activity

Creative and Performing Arts

111. Which of these is correct about how EC teachers should engage young children in art activities?
   a. Teachers should wait until children's fine motor skills are fully developed before doing art.
   b. Teachers should guide children in thorough exploration of art materials before processes.
   c. Teachers should give children art activities that support symbolic concept representation.
   d. Teachers should ensure that children explore art processes before creating art products.

112. An EC teacher has been giving the class activities all week in various subject areas, all related to the theme of space travel. For an art activity, which can the teacher do most appropriately to this theme?
   a. Assign the children a project of painting their self-portraits
   b. Give them various materials and textures in the same color
   c. Start a class discussion of what they know of space travel
   d. Assign the children the construction of model rocket ships

113. An EC teacher has written down a lesson plan for an art activity step by step. Which of the following steps should the teacher and students do last?
   a. Have a preliminary discussion about the activity
   b. Look at activity-related artworks and/or photos
   c. Set up the necessary materials and instruments
   d. Book sharing/reading related to the art activity

114. In addition to artistic functions, art within its context can serve physical, personal, and/or social functions. Which of the following examples has an artistic function but no physical function?
   a. An elegant raku bowl used in a Japanese tea ceremony
   b. A Dada artist's cup, saucer, and spoon covered with hair
   c. An exquisitely crafted tribal war club to beat the enemy
   d. Any and all of these examples serve a physical function

115. When a performer develops a personal concept of what the artwork to be performed is intended to achieve or express, this represents which step in the artistic performance process?
   a. Interpreting
   b. Analyzing
   c. Selecting
   d. Evaluating

116. This component of visual art is the path of a moving point, the outline of a solid, 3-D object, or the edge of a two-dimensional figure. It is longer than it is wide and may be straight, curved, wavy, angular, or zigzag; and horizontal, vertical, or diagonal. It can be there physically, or implied or suggested. Its movement is called direction; its placement is called location. It defines areas, and expresses different qualities through its characteristics to evoke different viewer responses. It is:
   a. Shape
   b. Line
   c. Color
   d. Form

117. Which of these is defined as a secondary color?
   a. Red
   b. Blue
   c. Purple
   d. Yellow

118. When musicians play or sing several notes of different pitches at the same time, this creates:
   a. Tempo.
   b. Rhythm.
   c. Melody.
   d. Harmony.

119. Of the following, which pair of terms are musical directions for rhythm rather than tempo?
   a. *Andante* and *lento*
   b. *Staccato* and *legato*
   c. *Allegro* and *adagio*
   d. *Largo* and *presto*

120. When we perceive a painting, song, dance, or play as cohesive, with all elements belonging together and combining to create a completely realized whole whereby the artist effectively communicates the mood, atmosphere, feeling, and story, this reflects the organizing principle of:
   a. Repetition
   b. Contrast
   c. Balance
   d. Unity

Answers and Explanations

Language and Literacy

1. A: Phonological awareness primarily involves knowing the sounds used in speaking one's native language. It also involves understanding the relationships between spoken and written language, but not primarily knowing *only* the letters (B), words (C), or spelling (D) of the language; phonology is focused on speech sounds.

2. D: Young children whose phonological awareness skills are developing well can typically do all of these: think about (A), talk about (B), and manipulate (C) phonemes (i.e., speech sounds); for example, they can change words by varying their component individual and combined phonemes.

3. C:.Typically, young children with normal development of phonological awareness skills can both recognize and produce rhyming words (A); separate words or syllables into their individual speech sounds/phonemes and also blend individual phonemes into syllables and words (B); change words into other words by substituting one phoneme for another (C); and also alter words by both adding and removing phonemes (D).

4. B: Research finds that preschool-aged children exhibiting delayed language development are more likely to receive diagnoses of reading disorders when they begin school, and that instruction in PPA helps them. PPA instruction is also found to help preschoolers with articulation (pronunciation) disorders (C) and school-aged children with spelling disorders (D). In fact, all children who are learning to read, including not just preschoolers but also kindergarteners and first-graders (A), benefit from instruction in PPA.

5. A: Phonics is an instructional method that establishes the Alphabetic Principle—that is, the concept that written/printed letters correspond to speech sounds—and teaches skills for decoding words, i.e., breaking words down into their individual sounds and letters, and encoding, i.e., combining/blending phonemes/letters to form words. Phonemic awareness (B) is awareness of the individual phonemes used in one's native language. Phonological awareness (C) is the general awareness of speech sounds, which infants and young children develop through hearing spoken language. Thus only (A) best fits the definition given, not all of these (D).

6. B: Morphology is the smallest structural units that determine grammatical differences in meaning, like the –s ending differentiating the singular noun *book* from the plural *books*. Phonology (A) is the rules for combining a language's phonemes or speech sounds into syllables and words. Syntax (C) is the ordering of words and structuring of word combinations to make grammatical sentences. Semantics (D) is the meanings of the words in a language.

7. C: Expert researchers have observed that teachers commonly tend to do most of the speaking in EC classrooms, but they should NOT; rather, they should focus on eliciting more conversational speech from the children. Experts advise teachers to describe the children's activities and actions (A) often; to make a habit of repeating children's utterances, adding some more information to their repetitions (B); and frequently to provide reflective comments on and descriptions of the properties of the concrete objects (D) encountered by the children.

8. D: Advanced Fluency is considered the fifth and final stage of ESL acquisition, typically achieved by students around five to seven years into their learning of English. Within about the first six

months (A), ESL students undergo the first, Preproduction stage. They typically reach the second stage, Early Production, about six months to one year into learning. They usually achieve the third, Speech Emergence stage within about one to three years into learning (B), and the fourth stage of Intermediate Fluency around three to five years into learning (C).

9. A: Stuttering is considered a speech disorder of rate and rhythm: it involves repetitions of phonemes, syllables, words, or short phrases; prolongations of phonemes; blocking of phonemes; faster and/or slower than normal ranges of speech; and disrupted/abnormal speech rhythms. Cleft palate (B), a birth defect wherein the hard palate and lip are split/not fused, can cause voice disorders like hypernasality, and articulation disorders. Jargon aphasia (C), often caused by brain injury, is characterized by repeating syllables ("cacacacaca," "nanananana," etc.) sounding like babbling when attempting to produce words. Motor apraxia (D), typically caused by brain damage/defects, can interfere with the ability to produce individual phonemes, and hence words.

10. D: Although a child whose parents do not provide adequate social and linguistic interactions is likely to suffer from low self-esteem, delayed language development, and other developmental deficits, low self-esteem levels do not specifically delay language development. For example, some children's parents interact and talk with them enough so they develop good self-esteem; but if the parents are linguistically and educationally deprived, their children may also show delayed language development. Developmental delays, including in language, are common among children with mental retardation (A), minimal neurological damage (B), and those environmentally deprived (C) of sufficient conversations, being read to, and other normal interactions that support language development.

11. B: Children cannot learn the sounds represented by printed/written letters, and cannot recognize printed words, without knowing the letters' names. Knowing letter names is closely correlated with being able to see words as combinations of letters and to remember printed words. Knowing the alphabet sequence (A) helps them remember all the letters, but by itself is not as important to learn letter-sound correspondences as being able to identify and name them. They must be able to write letters (C) to write words, sentences, and beyond, but not to learn sound-letter relationships or read words. They must learn both letter shapes and letter names (D) to recognize letters, learn letter sounds, and identify words.

12. C: To strengthen beginning preschoolers' alphabetic knowledge, teachers should not only review what children have learned cumulatively about letter-sound correspondences (A), and not only provide opportunities to practice letter-sound relationships they are newly learning (B), but should do both. One good way to provide occasions for children to apply their emerging alphabetic knowledge early and often is to give them phonetic spellings of words familiar to them (D) so they can read these.

13. B: The less proficient in English an ELL student is, the more dependent s/he will be on cues from their first/native language (L1). Spanish-speaking children do NOT learn to sound out words the same ways as English-speaking children (A). In English, students are taught phonics, the 1:1 relationship of each sound to the letter representing it. In Spanish, however, students are taught to sound out words by the syllable, not the letter. ELL students do NOT use the same amount of cognitive energy as native English speakers (C) to develop English-language literacy: they exert TWICE the cognitive effort in attending to new phonemes, structures, meanings, and literacy skills and concepts. Directionality is NOT the same across languages (D): while English and European languages go left-to-right, Hebrew and Arabic letters go right-to-left (but Arabic numbers go left-to-

right); and Chinese, Japanese, and Korean traditionally went top-to-bottom, but today may be vertical or horizontal.

14. D: Normally developing preschoolers typically develop print awareness skills that include all of these: reciting the alphabet; recognizing both printed letters and printed words; and using print as a vehicle for communication.

15. C: Having students retell a story that the teacher read with them is an excellent way to make an informal assessment of their comprehension. In Expanded Book Reading, it *is* advisable for teachers to give students summaries (A) or overviews of a book before reading, and also to ask students to predict what the book might be about (B). Teachers *can* use this method compatibly with integrating literacy across all curriculum (D) subjects, e.g., by planning art, music, math, and science activities using books they and students have read together.

16. B: In the 3N strategy, the Notice step does NOT involve having the student observe his/her own literacy strategies (A); it involves the teacher's observing the student's current literacy level. The Nudge step does involve the teacher's providing temporary support, i.e., scaffolding, to help the student achieve literacy tasks s/he could not yet accomplish independently. This scaffolding is gradually decreased as student proficiency levels increase. The Narrate step does NOT involve having the student verbally describe (C) or reflect on (D) his/her literacy activity; it involves the teacher verbally describing and reflecting on what the student did and accomplished during the activity.

17. A: Narrative writing is storytelling, as opposed to expository or informational writing. Ability to retell the story is a key strategy for assessing a student's reading comprehension. Decoding new words (B), inventing original spellings for new words (C), and identifying and producing rhymes (D) are all abilities whereby teachers can assess student skills for decoding printed words, but not their comprehension of printed text.

18. B: So-called "predictable books" are those that feature repetition throughout the text. This is an advantage, not a disadvantage, for young children learning to read, because the repetition affords familiarity, allowing children to participate immediately in the story and also to remember and practice words and language patterns. Predictability refers to repetition, not to a lack of plot originality (A) or imagination (C). In addition to immediate engagement and practice, repetitive texts *are* also naturally appealing to young children (D), who love repeating and hearing familiar words, rhymes, phrases, chants, songs, and stories repeated over and over.

19. C: *Winnie the Pooh* by A. A. Milne is the best example of modern fantasy children's literature: it is written by an original author, and it tells imaginary stories, often involving quests. *Old Possum's Book of Practical Cats* by T.S. Eliot (A) is an example of a book of poetry. Aesop's *Fables* (B) is an example of traditional literature, as are folklore, proverbs, and epics. *Lincoln: A Photobiography* by Russell Freedman (D) is an example of a non-fiction informational children's book (specifically, a read-aloud book with pictures).

20. D: If a child only looks at the first letter or two of a word and tries to guess at the word from this limited information, this is a sign that s/he could have difficulty with phonics, and with decoding words by their correspondence with the speech sounds they represent and vice versa {(A), (B)}. After the teacher instructs the class in several letter sounds, if a student then incorporates these in his or her writing (C), this is a sign that the student has mastered and is applying these, not having difficulty with them.

21. C: ESL students can understand the teacher's questions, as well as engage in informal conversations with peers and adults, using conversational English. However, in order to understand their school textbooks (A), solve mathematical word problems (B), and understand and communicate novel and/or abstract concepts (D) as well as write papers and reports, they must master academic English, which is more difficult.

22. B: A word wall typically includes not only the vocabulary words the teacher is targeting for young students to learn, but also synonyms (B) for these target words (D), and pictures (A) illustrating the concepts represented by the target words. Thus it has both words and pictures (C).

23. A: When a child's reading out loud sounds choppy and awkward, this is a sign that the child lacks reading fluency. To read fluently, children must not only sound fluent when reading aloud (B), but also read quickly, smoothly, and effortlessly when reading silently to achieve good comprehension and time-efficiency. When reading aloud, fluent readers not only read the words accurately, but also supply the appropriate expression (C) for the meanings in the text. Reading fluency is measured by *both* speed *and* accuracy (D) in reading.

24. B: Reading comprehension problems can be indicated by either or both: focusing on details to the exclusion of main concepts, i.e., "missing the forest for the trees," (A) can signal inadequate comprehension; but even when understanding the main ideas, being unable to relate any details (C) like a story's setting, characters' appearances, etc., can equally signify comprehension problems. Good comprehension enables both understanding the main points and also noticing and retaining supporting details. In addition, even if a student gets the main ideas, an inability to retell logical sequences of events in the reading (D) is a sign that the student's reading comprehension is deficient.

25. C: One sign that a child may have dyslexia is that, even though the child has good fine-motor skills and word-processing abilities, s/he still demonstrates poor handwriting. A common error among dyslexic students *is* to miss syllables within words (A): when reading aloud, they may say the word with one syllable omitted because they did not see it or could not decode it. Children with dyslexia not only often misspell words, but also often confuse words that sound similar (B) [e.g., *volcano/tornado*]. Due to previous unsuccessful experiences and expectations of making errors, students with dyslexia typically are *un*willing to read aloud (D) and try to avoid it.

26. D: Five stages of spelling identified (Gentry, 1982) are: Precommunicative; Semiphonetic; Phonetic; Transitional; and Correct. In the Phonetic stage, children represent all the speech sounds they hear in words with written letters. While their spelling in this stage is not always correct, it is nonetheless applied systematically and understandable to others. Children in the fifth, Correct (A) stage usually spell words accurately and recognize misspellings. In the fourth, Transitional (B) stage, children begin moving from using phonetic spellings to conventional ones. In the second, Semiphonetic (C) stage, children are just beginning to represent sounds with corresponding letters. (In the first, Precommunicative stage, children may use alphabet letters, but do not yet show understanding of letter-sound correspondences.)

27. C: Linguistic researchers have concluded from their studies of young children's invented spellings that spelling is a developmental process that leads to comprehension beyond simply memorizing word spellings (A) or knowing simply that letters correspond to sounds (B). One basis for this conclusion is the finding that diverse individual children all choose the same phonetic spellings, rather than choices varying individually (D). Such universal phonetic spelling choices

reflect young children's recognition of the phonetic properties in words, and of the roles of real spellings in symbolizing these properties.

28. B: Five identified stages of children's writing development are: Scribbling and drawing, wherein children first start using writing/drawing implements to explore line, form, and space; Letter-like forms and shapes (C), wherein they understand that writing can symbolize meaning, and begin drawing figures and shapes even if they do not know what they signify; Letters (D), wherein they can form letters but write them randomly without correspondence to speech sounds, which they eventually develop; Letters and spaces (B), wherein they understand the word concept, space correctly between words, correctly write word-initial and word-final letters and vowels, correctly spell some often-used words, and experiment with constructing and punctuating sentences; and Conventional writing and spelling (A), wherein children largely construct, spell, and punctuate accurately and write purposefully.

29. A: Literacy research finds that not only do enhanced reading skills improve students' writing skills, but enhancing their writing skills will also improve their reading skills, so the effects are mutual rather than one-way (D). Studies show that even normally developing students will not simply learn to write well on their own (B); they require instruction to become good writers. Improving student writing skills additionally *is* found, like improving reading skills, to enhance students' general capacity for learning (C).

30. B: POWER stands for Planning, Organization, Writing, Editing, and Rewriting. In the Planning (B) step, the student and teacher confirm that the student has selected an appropriate topic, has researched or read about it, considered which information on the topic the audience would want to read, and written down all his/her ideas. In the Organization (A) step, the teacher and student determine if the student grouped similar ideas, chose the best ideas for the composition, and sequenced them logically. In the Writing (C) step, teacher and student determine if the student used complete sentences, and asked someone for help and/or looked things up if needed. In the Editing (D) step, they confirm the student read his/her first draft, marking needed changes and parts s/he liked; and read it to a classmate/partner and considered the other's feedback. Rewriting involves student revisions in content and mechanics, and copying the final draft in his/her best handwriting.

31. C: Typically, young children learning to write develop the skill of writing two or more related sentences, using punctuation, before they develop the skill of writing separate paragraphs. The sequence is: letters, words, phrases (A), sentences (B), punctuation (D), and paragraphs (C).

32. D: Educational research has found that traditionally, most teachers have had the habit of evaluating student writing on the basis of its appearance and form more than its effectiveness and functionality. Educators now find that this focus on form is superficial, and diverts teacher attention from attending to the function of the writing and how effective it is at conveying meaning. However, because inadequate form undermines readers' first impressions of writing, teachers should balance their assessments between form and function (C) rather than focusing on function alone {(A), (B)}.

33. D: Both B, punctuation, and C, capitalization. The W in Washington and both initials D and C should be capitalized as it is a proper name; a comma should follow "Washington" and "D.C." should have periods after both initials (punctuation). These are not grammatical (A) errors, which involve such errors as subject-verb disagreement, incorrect verb tenses, dangling participles, misplaced modifiers, incorrect word order, etc.

34. C: A dangling participle is an example of an error in grammar rather than in handwriting. (For example, the sentence "While growing up, my parents taught me...." has a dangling participle or misplaced modifier: the modifier refers to the object [me], not the subject [my parents].) Examples of student errors in handwriting include incorrect or poor alignment (A) of letters, words, and/or lines; incorrect spacing (B) between letters and/or words; and writing illegibly (D), i.e., readers cannot decipher what letters/words were intended by the writer.

35. B: When teachers model for children and guide them in writing questions, reading them to ask classmates in "interviewing" them, and writing up their responses, this promotes children's motivation to write by connecting writing to familiar people and topics, and by providing an activity they find exciting and/or interesting. To motivate young children to write, teachers should also provide them with opportunities to practice evaluating authors and books first, until they eventually learn to write their own critiques—not vice versa (A). Experts advise teachers to make some deliberate errors when transcribing children's dictation (C) to give children opportunities to identify and correct the errors. They also recommend that teachers both bring in samples of their own writing and also invite children to do the same (D).

36. A: Research finds that among the motivational factors of self-efficacy—students' goal orientation for task performance and/or skills mastery (B); their interest and the value they perceive in a writing task (C); and to what causes they attribute their failures and/or successes in writing (D)—students' perceived competence, i.e., their sense of self-efficacy, for overall writing skills influences their motivation to write more than their respective self-efficacy for individual writing tasks.

Mathematics

37. B: It is vital for young children and all students to learn the concept that one problem can have multiple and various solutions in order to develop good problem-solving skills. This applies to solving math problems: not all math questions have only one possible right answer (A). Developing problem-solving skill is crucial to *all* parts of mathematics, not only certain ones (C). Mathematical and educational experts have found that problem-solving skills must be learned by doing, through much practice, and cannot be mastered without this practice (D).

38. D: As adults, we know that one cookie, whether whole or broken into two pieces, is the same amount. However, as Piaget showed, young children who have not yet developed the cognitive ability to perform (mathematical or logical) mental operations do not know this. They focus ("centrate") on one aspect, e.g., the number of pieces, and fail to "conserve" the idea of an amount despite its appearance, division, or arrangement. Knowing the concepts of having three toys (A), of representing a number of objects symbolically with the corresponding number of fingers (B), and of addition, e.g., $2 + 1 = 3$ using concrete objects like cookies (C), are all better examples of a young child's using mathematical concepts.

39. A: When adults play mental math games with young children, like those involving story problems, experts advise that this not be a one-way process: the adult and child should take turns so the child views the game as fair and reciprocal. When it is the child's turn to pose the problem, the adult must try to solve it, even when the child uses invented numbers (e.g., "gazillion"). It is more important for adults to ask questions of children than to give them the answers (B). Math games with young children should be fun for them, rather than being strictly factual like math tests

(C). Young children should NOT be given unknown variable/number games while still in early childhood (D), as these are usually too abstract for them to understand until they are about five to six years old.

40. C: Piaget identified very young children's thinking as "preoperational", i.e., not yet formal (A), logical (B), or using hypothetical or deductive (D) processes. Rather, he labeled their thinking as intuitive. Young children naturally learn to use intuitive mathematical thought as they encounter and learn to solve everyday problems in their real-life experiences. They typically only develop formal, logical, and deductive mathematical thinking via the maturation of middle childhood and several years of formal education.

41. B: To help children learn to apply formal math to solving real-life, everyday problems, teachers need to establish connections between the intuitive mathematical thinking that preschool children naturally use. To do this, they should *not* emphasize a view of math as a group of rules and procedures (A): this is how children beginning school often come to view formal math, and it *prevents* them from realizing they can apply it to real life for solving problems. Teachers can, however, help children see connections between their natural problem-solving mathematical processes and the math they are learning in school, by providing concrete objects familiar to children that they can manipulate to work through math problems (C), because young children think concretely, and using concrete manipulatives helps them understand abstract concepts and prepares them for progressing to abstract thought. Teachers can also illustrate math concepts using real-life examples relevant to children's real-life experiences (D), and describe children's activities using math vocabulary words, allowing children to realize how they naturally use mathematical operations (D).

42. D: This activity applies the mathematical concepts of conservation of liquid volume (A), i.e., the understanding that the same amount of liquid remains the same despite the size and/or shape of the container holding it; of measurement (B) when they test their speculations by observing how many ounces of liquid each container holds; and of estimation (C) when they guess how much a container will hold or whether a given amount will fit into a given container before actually trying it.

43. C: Children develop symbolic representation early, as when they play creating "make-believe"/"pretend" scenarios. Counting on their fingers (B) is another early example of emerging math skills. Once they can control writing implements beyond scribbling, they may keep counts of things or events by make written tallies using tick-marks (D), check-marks, and even words once they are able to write these. Young children will also represent things by drawing pictures of them, and drawing simple maps (A) of places and/or directions—involving real-life locations and also make-believe ones, as with "pirate" treasure maps. Children will progress to making graphs (C) to depict numbers of things/people/events, intervals of time, and relationships, when they are older.

44. A: By asking the child to come up with alternative criteria for sorting (e.g., by size, shape, or weight instead of by color), the teacher is helping the child to develop problem-solving skills in thinking of a variety of alternative solutions/answers. Telling the child that by sorting, s/he is performing classification (B) is a better example of teaching formal math vocabulary by connecting it with informal math activity, rather than of promoting problem solving. Asking the child how s/he is sorting the rocks (C) is a better example of promoting math communication through explaining the sorting criterion, rather than promoting problem solving. Therefore, answer choice (D) is incorrect.

45. D: We tend not only to see or impose patterns and relationships where they do not objectively exist (like seeing animal, human, and object shapes in the clouds); we also deliberately create patterns and relationships in the works of art (A), pieces of music (B), and articles of clothing (C) we produce. We also notice and appreciate the patterns and relationships in these products that others have created.

46. C: Once children understand patterns and relationships in general, they can then understand how to categorize things because they comprehend the relationships of shared characteristics, e.g., these are all vegetables, these are all animals, etc. Understanding patterns IS related to children's understanding repetition (A), because patterns consist of regular repetitions. Patterns and relationships also DO inform understanding of rhythm (B)—e.g., differentiating longer/shorter durations of sounds or movements, identifying patterns of repeating and alternating durations, etc. This understanding IS the knowledge that enables children to order things from smallest to largest, shortest to longest (D), etc., because they comprehend the relationships that this is smaller/bigger than that, etc.

47. B: When a child counts how many dots of one color there are in a fabric print before a different color is used, this activity is focused on identifying the pattern(s) in the print. Stringing beads with different colors in a pre-selected order (A), arranging and gluing down pieces of alternating sizes (C), and hopping on each foot for pre-determined different numbers of times (D) are all activities that are focused on *creating*, rather than *identifying*, patterns.

48. A: Young children's number sense includes, but is not limited to, understanding that we use numbers to communicate information (B), to manipulate (work with) information (C), *and* to describe quantities of things and relationships between/among things (D). Therefore, number sense encompasses understanding all of these applications of numbers.

49. A: Adults can help young children develop numeracy skills, including number sense, by counting aloud and inviting children to count with them; by helping children sort objects by their similarities and differences in color, shape, size, etc.; and by discussing with children our uses of numbers, such as keeping score when playing games and finding street addresses and house/apartment numbers. When helping young children, adults *should* count on their own fingers and also encourage children to do the same (B). Young children will need their fingers until they develop enough proficiency and abstraction to count mentally. When counting a series of objects, both adults and children *should* point to each object (C) as they count it. Like using fingers, this affords counting practice that young children need. When young children repeat or skip numbers while counting, adults *should* help them to count without such repetitions or omissions (D).

50. B: Among the activities listed, the first one that adults can best do with young children is to identify the names of various shapes, figures, and angles for them, since they are not likely to start out already knowing these. *After* supplying these names for children to learn, adults can then ask them later to name these figures when they see them (A). Once they are familiar with names for shapes, figures, angles, etc., adults can ask them to trace over drawings of these with their fingers (C) before they have the children actually draw these forms themselves (D).

51. C: Allowing young children to crawl or climb into and out of big boxes, climb over furniture, and navigate into, out of, under, over, around, and through various real structures and objects will help them to understand the relationships of their bodies to solid forms and empty spaces, providing a good conceptual foundation for geometry. This direct physical experience is more effective for this

learning than drawing pictures of objects (A), matching objects to pictures of them (B), or taking photographs of objects (D), which are all more abstract and less concrete.

52. D: An effective way to help young children develop early math skills related to measurement is to ask them to help with everyday chores and activities that incorporate measurement—e.g., shopping, cooking, sewing, gardening, etc.—and use these activities to discuss measurement concepts and processes with the children as they participate directly, which is more effective than if they only watch the adult demonstrate (C). Adults should *not* discourage young children from using their own personal units of measurement (A); this is a natural and useful practice, as when a child says his friend is as tall as four teddy bears. Adults can moreover apply this practice to describe measurements in ways young children can understand better than if they tried to teach them standardized units of measurement in isolated lessons (B) with no real-life referents.

53. D: Piaget demonstrated that young children are not yet able to perform and reverse abstract mental operations, including the logic of understanding fractions, e.g., pieces of a cookie vs. a whole cookie. Preoperational children focus on one rather than all properties of an object. Therefore, when they see four pieces compared to one whole cookie, they "centrate" and focus on the number of pieces rather than the total amount, commonly concluding that four pieces equal more cookie than the same amount in one piece. They do not recognize that, whether whole or cut up, both cookies are equal amounts (A). They typically do not see the single cookie as equaling more than the four pieces (B). Though they do not think logically, they do base intuitive decisions on appearance, and hence do not conclude that a quarter-piece of cookie is as much as the whole cookie (C).

54. C: Adults can help young children gain an informal understanding of fractions by engaging them in real-life everyday activities involving dividing up and sharing parts of things like a pan of brownies. Having children compare the sizes of their pizza slices (A) teaches size comparisons of bigger/smaller, but not fractions (i.e., dividing things into equally sized parts). Asking young children to divide beads into different proportions like 1/6, 2/6, and 3/6 (B) is too abstract for them; this represents an exercise in *formal* (not informal) math fractions more appropriate for older children who have learned some academic math. Asking young children which apple is bigger, a whole one or one cut into halves (D), requires a later stage of cognitive development: preoperational children will likely say the halves equal more because there are two pieces, while the whole apple is only one piece.

55. B: Adults can give young children experience and practice with estimation by asking them to guess quantities—for example, which of their playmates is tallest—and then make an actual measurement to test the child's guess for reference. Repeated experience with comparing guesses to real measures will help children learn to make realistic estimates. Adults should also consistently incorporate vocabulary words indicating estimation (e.g., "near," "more than/less than," "around/about/approximately," "between," etc.) in their everyday conversations (A) with children. Adults should model estimating for children when it is appropriate, rather than always using only exact measurements to describe quantities (C). In helping young children learn to estimate, adults should not aim for children to attain precise quantities (D), but rather to make estimates that are close to reality.

56. A: A calendar is one type of chart. We use charts and graphs to organize information, interpret it, and more readily visualize relationships within the information. Using calendars can help the youngest children understand how information is organized by showing them this organization visually in graphic form. Statistical tables showing differences among groups (B) or individuals are

- 73 -

commonly used by scientists to present the results of their research studies, but are not as appropriate for very young children. Line graphs (C) are better for depicting changes over time. Weather forecasts (D) are better for helping children understand basically how scientists predict probabilities, i.e., the chances something will happen.

57. A: Dividing a chart by color and having each child place his/her chosen color of sticker onto a chart divided with a section for each color is the best example to show them how they can organize and display data (represented by stickers) they have collected. Having each child differentiate among shapes (B) is a better example of helping them to learn the properties of different figures. Having them guess how many stickers of each color were chosen (C) is a better example of teaching them intuitive concepts of predicting probabilities. Having each child get a sticker for being on time and a reward for accumulating five consecutive stickers (D) is an example of the behaviorist method of using a token economy to reinforce desired behaviors.

58. B: By having the children sort objects according to their similarities and differences in properties like size, texture, etc., the teacher is supporting the math concept of classifying, also known as categorizing or sorting. The children are learning to group things according to common properties, and to separate groups that differ in the properties they share. Patterning (A) would be better supported by an activity in which they arrange objects with alternating properties—e.g., stringing three blue beads, then one yellow, then three blue, etc. Counting (C) would involve things like pointing to each object, identifying it by number "One, two, three…," and stating the total number of objects, rather than sorting them. Ordering (D) would be supported by activities wherein children arrange objects in a sequence from biggest to smallest or vice versa, or longest to shortest, etc., rather than grouping them.

59. C: Understanding of and familiarity with relationships and patterns is most applicable to an activity that requires children to classify objects into sets or categories based on some property they share in common, like their color, size, shape, texture, use, etc. Determining which group has more objects (A) is an activity that requires understanding and familiarity with counting and comparison. Comparing three-dimensional object shapes with two-dimensional shapes (B) also requires experience with comparisons, as well as the ability to generalize between solid objects and flat representations. Matching written numbers with their values (D) requires understanding symbolic representation and familiarity with counting and number names.

60. D: Math education experts believe that when children can count to twenty, thirty, etc., to one hundred, they begin to discover the first consistent mathematical pattern they observe, that of base ten (i.e., twenty = two tens, thirty = three tens, etc., and we add only numbers from one to nine before reaching the next set of tens). Learning to count from one to twelve involves memorization, but NOT more unusual rules (A). Counting from thirteen to nineteen *does* involve less regular rules, in addition to the same amount of memorizing, NOT more (B). However, learning to count above twenty actually involves *more* consistent rules (C), and these facilitate children's recognition of the base ten pattern.

61. D: This activity engages both analysis of shapes—i.e., knowing that a triangle has three sides, and that those sides may or may not be equal in length—and also naming, in that the adult tells the children the name of the shape to find, so they must know what a triangle is to find it *without* relying on its appearance {(A), (B)} since they were told to close their eyes and find it by touch. Thus the activity does not engage *only* analysis (C).

62. C: Traditionally, EC teachers have followed the approach of always taking advantage of "teachable moments" in everyday preschool/school activities (A). For example, when children line up for going outside, choosing teams, or other activities, teachers have them practice counting with cardinal and ordinal numbers ("one, two.../first, second...."). However, more recently, educators advise that using such natural opportunities alone is insufficient, especially with larger classes, and that using such opportunities *cannot* be applied systematically (D), as by nature they occur spontaneously and cannot be planned. They find that using a curriculum (or combining several, or selecting parts of several) affords a more planned approach. However, these experts also recommend *both* curriculum planning *and* utilizing naturally occurring opportunities to integrate math into all daily EC activities.

63. B: Performing mental operations—i.e., figuring out logical processes in one's mind without any physical referents—is a cognitive development children typically do not attain until they are older, e.g., around middle-school ages. Younger children do naturally learn basic math concepts as they normally explore their environments (A). However, until they develop mental operations at later ages, young children need concrete objects to manipulate (C) to engage their more concrete thinking so they can comprehend mathematical concepts. As they learn through hands-on exploration of their environments and the discoveries they make, young children observe real-life relationships (D), e.g., that objects have similarities and differences, that things can be put into categories based on these, and that patterns, both natural and man-made, exist in life.

64. A: When young children develop spatial awareness—i.e., understanding how their own bodies move through space and in relationship to other people and objects, and the relationships among objects and within space—this helps them also to develop their gross motor skills, physical coordination, *and* social skills. Fine motor skills {(B), (C), (D)} are developed more by activities involving small, coordinated movements of the hands and fingers and manipulating small objects, instruments, utensils, etc.

65. B: Fitting simplified jigsaw puzzle pieces together most demonstrates the early math skill of understanding relationships of parts to the whole. It does not require measuring (A) the pieces or the whole. It does not involve analyzing data (C), such as counting how many things fit into each of several categories. And solving the puzzles requires understanding how the shapes fit together, rather than identifying patterns (D), i.e., a regular arrangement of the forms using repetition and organization.

66. C: Numbers such as zip codes, area codes, etc., are nominal numbers: they are used as names to identify things, but they do not represent mathematical number values, numerical quantities, or mathematical operations. "Second" (A) is an ordinal number: it indicates the order something/someone takes within a group, set, series, or sequence. "Seven" (B) is a cardinal number: it indicates how many, or the quantity of something. 3.141592... (D), i.e., the value of pi (π), is an irrational (endlessly continuing beyond the decimal point) number; as such, it is a real number. Real numbers include all rational and irrational numbers (cardinal or not).

Social Studies

67. D: Identification is the third of five progressive levels of self-awareness that children develop. In differentiation (B), the first level, children can distinguish their mirrored images from other people, and realize that their reflection's movements correspond to their own movements. In situation (C), the second level, children then realize their mirror images are unique to themselves

and that their bodies and selves are situated in space. In identification (D), the third level, children identify their reflections as "me." When they see something on their reflected faces, they know to touch their faces rather than the mirror to touch or remove the object. In permanence (A), the fourth level, children realize their self is permanent over time and space, recognizing themselves in photos and videos regardless of their ages, clothing, location, etc. (The fifth level is self-consciousness or "meta"-self-awareness, i.e., seeing oneself from others' as well as one's own perspective.)

68. C: Babies typically develop the self-awareness ability to differentiate between live video of themselves and people imitating their behaviors around four to seven months of age. Newborns (A) demonstrate the self-awareness ability of differentiating their bodies from the environment and internal/self from external/other stimulation from birth. Two-year-olds (B) demonstrate awareness of symbolic representation, understanding that mirror images and photos represent themselves. Babies typically regularly reach for things they see around four months of age. Around four to six months (D) of age, babies are able to regulate their reaching movements according to their postural and balance levels.

69. B: Most infants typically develop the behavior of sharing activities with their peers, most notably activities involving toys or other concrete objects, by the age of one year. They have usually developed the motor and cognitive skills to walk and talk by the time they are two years old, enabling them to coordinate their behaviors while they play with their peers (A). From around three to five years old, children's development of the understanding of symbolic representation increases, as evidenced by their increasing engagement in "make-believe" scenarios (D) and pretend play. So, too, do their prosocial behaviors of helping and caring for others (C) increase during this early childhood period.

70. A: After approaching calmly, stopping any behaviors that cause physical or emotional harm (step 1), and acknowledging the children's feelings (step 2), the third step in this conflict-mediation/resolution process* is to accumulate as much information as is necessary about the particular conflict from the involved parties. The fourth step is for the mediator to reiterate or restate what the problem is (C). The fifth step is to ask the involved children to think of and suggest potential solutions to the problem identified, and then help them agree to one selected solution (B). The sixth step is to follow up the conflict resolution by providing the involved parties with whatever support they need (D). *[from the HighScope Educational Research Foundation]

71. B: Permissive parents are nurturing, responsive, and communicative with their children. However, they avoid confronting and/or disciplining children and do not expect them to demonstrate much self-control or maturity. Consequently, their children tend to have problems with authority figures, poor school performance, and deficits in self-regulation. The children of unresponsive, overly strict, demanding, harshly punitive authoritarian (A) parents tend to develop proficient technical and school performance and obedience, but lack social skills, self-esteem, and happiness. The children of authoritative (C) parents, who have the ideal parenting style, tend to develop competence, success, and happiness. Uninvolved (D) parents, who are undemanding but also unresponsive, uncommunicative, and detached, and may even neglect or reject children, produce children lacking competence, self-esteem, and self-control.

72. C: In family systems theory, the family climate refers to the family's physical and emotional environment and emotional quality. Climate affects a child's feelings of safety or fear, support or rejection, and feeling loved or unloved. Hierarchy (A) refers to the family's balance of power, decision making, and control, which can change with changes in family makeup and is affected by

factors like socioeconomic status, age, gender, religion, and culture. Boundaries (B) refer to the family's limits and definitions of togetherness and separateness, and what the family excludes or includes. Equilibrium (D) refers to the family's consistency or balance, which is preserved through family customs, traditions, and rituals, and disrupted by changes and stressors.

73. D: Individualistic cultures, like that of the United States, value scientific thinking and object manipulation as skills to teach young children. Individualism favors the independence of each person, individuals realizing their full potential (self-actualization), and distinguishing themselves from the group. Collectivism favors the interdependence (C) of individuals and their social relationships, interactions, and connections. Collectivist cultures value cooperation to achieve group harmony (B), while individualist cultures value competition among group members to achieve individual excellence.

74. C: Both culturally diverse families and American educators experience equal problems in their interactions. Educators and diverse families both have difficulties dealing with foreign languages, different customs and behaviors, and major differences in the educational systems with which they are familiar—including different laws for special education. Thus neither the families (A) nor the educators (B) experience greater difficulty than the other. Moreover, the challenges both groups experience are not necessarily or even usually very minimal (D) in nature; they can be quite substantial.

75. B: Researchers have found that Hispanic families in the U.S. are more likely to choose home- and family-based child care and preschool education than outside centers. This may reflect the collectivist nature of Latin culture, which values social interactions and relationships more than structure. Caucasian parents in the U.S. are found to prefer preschool centers. This reflects not only the North American culture's individualistic emphasis on structured early learning, and predominant North American custom, but also North American Caucasian parents' attention to scientific findings that center-based preschool education improves children's school readiness skills.

76. A: Researchers find that having differing cultural values (B) is not the only or main factor influencing how much parents in the U.S. from different cultures read to their children. In addition to cultural values, temporal and economic limitations (C), parental literacy levels—both in their native languages and in English as a second language (D)—and other factors as well, influence parental behaviors of reading to their children.

77. B: One factor educators must consider about immigrant parents is that they may not be aware of what special education and/or supplemental services are available to their children in American schools. Thus they are not negligent or refusing to request such services, but need to be informed about them, which educators must do. Culturally diverse parents and educators are likely to disagree about some educational goals for children, but educators should collaborate with parents to further those goals they both agree on rather than trying to convince parents to agree (A) on all goals. Educators should also remember that immigrant parents' not advocating for their children to receive needed services is not necessarily due to lack of interest (C) or resistance to confronting problems (D). In addition to lacking information, some parents from cultures with more paternalistic educational systems are trained *not* to speak up, but to wait for educators to raise concerns before expressing children's problems they have witnessed.

78. C: Research has found significant variations among parental age expectations for various EC developmental milestones (e.g., weaning, eating, toilet-training, dressing, sleeping, etc.). Thus what

is normal for one culture is abnormal for another. For example, Anglo parents usually introduce and encourage drinking from a cup to one-year-olds, so an eighteen-month-old not doing this could signal some developmental delay; but Filipino parents normally have not even introduced a cup to eighteen-month-olds, so their not using cups is developmentally normal. As in this example, some developmental milestones not reached by a certain age is *not* always a cause for concern (D). Assessment data *are* more likely to be misinterpreted when the educators' and parents' cultures differ (A) than when they share a common culture. Although age expectations for milestones vary across cultures, educators *cannot* automatically attribute everything to this variation when a child could also need a complete developmental assessment (B).

79. D: Area differentiation in geography refers to regional variations in occupations. It also refers to regional variations in geographical characteristics; e.g., people grow different plants in highlands than in lowlands according to what grows best in their respective altitudes and climates. (A) is an example of the geographical concept of utility value, i.e., how much use natural resources are to different people—oceans have more utility value for fishermen than farmers, while forests have more utility value for naturalists than academics. (B) is an example of the geographical concept of spatial interrelatedness, i.e., the relationship of geographic phenomena and non-physical characteristics like rural or urban regions. (C) is an example of the geographical concept of agglomeration, i.e., the tendency of people and their settlements and activities to concentrate in the most profitable areas.

80. A: A political map is drawn to indicate the locations and boundaries of countries, regions within countries, and cities. A physical map (B) is drawn to show natural features like mountains, rivers, and lakes. A thematic map (C) is drawn to focus on a specific theme, like average rainfall in a certain area or the locations and names of battles in a certain war. A semantic map (D) is not a cartographic type. It commonly refers to a graphic organizer used as a literacy instruction strategy to show related words in categories visually.

81. B: A line graph is the most common choice for representing visually the changes in quantities over time, because the line connecting the data points shows how the points rise or fall with each time period. A bar graph can also show differences across time, by having each bar represent the quantity of something at a given time, e.g., the amount of rainfall in a city each month. A pie chart {(A), (C)} clearly visualizes different proportions or percentages of a whole for easy comparison, but typically does not display changes over time. A column of numbers {(A), (D)} does not depict data visually like a picture, making them easier to see, the way that graphs do.

82. C: By the time students are in middle school grades, they should be able to measure time mathematically, e.g., years, decades, centuries, and millennia. They should also be able to interpret data displayed on time lines by middle school, not high school (A). Middle school students, not high school students, should also be able to calculate time in B.C. and B.C. (D). By the time they are in high school, not middle school, students should be able to analyze patterns of historical duration (B) and historical succession.

83. D: EC teachers can assign children to small groups to make class rules, and then to revise them to be more realistic. For example, children might make a rule of "No talking" and then revise it to say "Listen when others talk" and/or "Speak softly in class." EC teachers need not limit their materials to non-fiction; creative teachers have successfully illustrated citizenship concepts via children's literature (A). This is effective because children personally identify with story characters, and the situations in the stories are cognitively appropriate for making citizenship concepts concrete and real to children (B). Fictional narratives can also serve as springboards for

starting discussions with young children about when rules do or do not apply. This method can often engage their interest and comprehension more than simply reading actual rules (C).

Science

84. D: When babies/toddlers build by putting together blocks and then take them apart again, they are learning about part-to-whole relationships. When they observe that some objects roll away while others do not (A), they are learning about shapes. When infants awaken wet and hungry and then are changed and fed (B), they are already beginning to learn about time and temporal sequences. When they crawl or climb under, into, onto, and around furniture (C), they are developing spatial sense.

85. C: Although preschool children do spontaneously initiate naturalistic activities to explore their environment, it is not true that adults need not add anything (A). Children need adult feedback to inform, and positive reinforcement to reward, children when their actions are appropriate (e.g., when they correctly identify something as "big," "little," "heavy," etc.). Since children do spontaneously initiate activities that appeal to their curiosity and enjoyment, adults should NOT choose and overtly direct them to engage in specific activities (B). Though children are naturally motivated by their curiosity and by novel things, adults DO need to supply them with ample materials (D) for sensory exploration, i.e., things and substances they can see, hear, touch, smell, and taste.

86. B: The first step in the scientific method is to ask a research question to which we want to find an answer. The second step is to formulate a hypothesis (A), which is an educated guess about the answer to the research question. The third step is to conduct an experiment (C) to test the hypothesis. The final steps are to decide whether the results of the experiment prove or disprove the hypothesis, and then to report this to others (D).

87. A: Water vapor is a gas, i.e., the gaseous form of water, which is a liquid (C) at normal temperatures. Vapors are gaseous forms of substances that are liquids or solids (B) at normal temperatures. They form through evaporation and/or heating. Cooling water vapor makes it liquid; freezing liquid water makes it into ice, a solid. Therefore (D) is incorrect.

88. A: These six gases are known as noble gases because the outer shells of their molecules contain complete sets of electrons, while other gases have either incomplete or excessive electrons in their outer shells. Their complete electron sets make noble gases very stable, not unstable (B). The noble gases are all elementary gases, i.e., made up of only one chemical element. Compound gases (C) are made up of more than one element. Therefore, (D) is also incorrect.

89. B: The planet Earth is itself a gigantic magnet; its magnetism is the reason that compasses always point north. *All* electric motors, not just some (A), contain magnets. Tape recorders (C) contain magnets, and the tapes they play are magnetized. Loudspeakers and telephones (D), as well as generators, all operate using magnets.

90. C: Magnetic domains are groups of molecules that work as magnets, according to twentieth-century physicist Pierre Weiss's theory of magnetism. This theory states that these molecules are randomly arranged *until* they are magnetized, but then are no longer random (A) as they all align with the lines of force in the magnetic field affecting them. Physicists working more recently with

- 79 -

Weiss's theory *have* attributed the magnetism of these domains to the spinning of electrons (B) in their atoms. Today Weiss's theory is still widely accepted and has not been discredited (D).

91. D: When the electrons are strongly bound to the atoms of a substance, these atoms seldom release their electrons and thus do not conduct electricity well; such materials are electrical insulators—e.g., air, wood, glass, plastic, cotton, and ceramics. Metals and other substances whose atoms have free electrons that can separate from the atoms and move about are electrical conductors; electrical current flows freely through materials with loose electrons.

92. C: Heat sinks are included in many electronic devices, e.g., computers. Heat sinks are passive thermal exchange components that move heat away from parts it can damage, and dissipate it into the air via fans. The other choices are imaginary.

93. B: "Force equals mass times acceleration" is Newton's Second Law of Motion. Newton's First Law of Motion (A) states that an object at rest tends to stay at rest, and an object in motion to stay in motion, unless an opposing force changes that state of rest or motion. Newton's Third Law of Motion (C) states that for every action there is an equal and opposite reaction. Since (B) is correct, (D) is incorrect.

94. A: When sound waves reach us, our outer ears (B) receive and transmit them to the middle ears (C), which amplify and transmit them to our inner ears, which convert the acoustic energy to electrical energy. Nerves transmit this energy to the brain, where certain parts of the brain (D) associated with hearing interpret the energy as sound.

95. B: The Earth rotates on its axis and revolves or orbits around the Sun. One complete *rotation* of the Earth on its axis equals one day (A) as we measure it. One complete *revolution* of the Earth around the Sun equals one year as we measure it. Months (C) are not associated with Earth's movements relative to the sun, but have been associated with the moon's phases as a satellite orbiting the Earth by those using lunar calendars. (The calendar most of us currently use features months slightly longer than lunar phases.) The Earth takes a year, not 100 years or a century (D), to orbit the Sun once.

96. C: Chemical sedimentary rocks are formed from deposits of minerals, as when flooding introduces water, which has minerals dissolved in it, and then the water evaporates, leaving behind layers of precipitated minerals no longer in solution without the water. Limestone is a chemical sedimentary rock, as are gypsum and rock salt. Clastic (A) sedimentary rock forms from clasts or little bits of rock that are compacted and cemented together. Organic (B) sedimentary rock forms from organic material like calcium from the bones and shells of animals. Pegmatite (D) is not a type of sedimentary rock; it is an intrusive igneous rock formed underground from cooling volcanic magma.

97. D: Living organisms change their behaviors according to internal cues, such as hunger, thirst, need for sunlight, need to reproduce, etc., and external cues like environmental changes, such as changes in temperature, amounts of water, availability of nutrients, etc. Their behavior is shaped NOT primarily by one or the other of these {(A), (B)} but by both. It is not controlled solely by genetic programming (C), but consists of adaptations to intrinsic needs and extrinsic changes in the environment.

98. D: A complete metamorphosis, as butterflies undergo, includes the stages of egg (A), larva (B), pupa (D), and imago (C) or adult form. Insects such as mosquitos, grasshoppers, dragonflies, and

cockroaches undergo an incomplete metamorphosis: they do not go through the stage of a pupa, which is typically inactive, does not feed, and stays hidden until the adult (imago) stage. The butterfly pupa, protected by a cocoon, is called a chrysalis. The mosquito pupa is called a tumbler.

99. C: The gametes are sperm and ova (eggs) in humans and other animals, and similar haploid (having one set of chromosomes) cells in plants. Plant gonads are gametophytes; animal gonads are the testes and ovaries. Both produce gametes through meiosis, the process of sexual reproduction producing cells with half the chromosomes, which then mate. Mitosis {(A), (D)} is the process of asexual reproduction whereby exact genetic copies are produced. Zygotes {(B), (D)} are diploid, formed through the combining of haploid gametes during fertilization.

100. B: In mutualistic ecological relationships, both involved organisms receive a benefit. For example, bacteria living in termites' digestive systems break down the cellulose in the wood that the termites eat, which the termites' digestive systems alone cannot do. In return for this nutritional aid, the bacteria receive a home and nourishment from the termites. In commensalistic relationships (A), one involved organism benefits while the other is unaffected; e.g., barnacles on whales are aided in their filter-feeding by the currents created in the water by the whales' swimming, while the whales are neither harmed nor helped by the barnacles. In parasitic relationships (C), one organism benefits but the other suffers. Common examples include fleas and tapeworms, which derive nourishment from animals, but harm the animals by robbing them of blood (fleas) and nutrition (tapeworms) and causing tissue damage and discomfort. Therefore (D) is incorrect.

Health and Physical Education

101. A: The goals of HHS' Community Program include decreasing secondhand smoke exposure, decreasing tobacco use, improving nutrition, reducing prevalence of obesity and overweight, and increasing amounts of physical activity. They do NOT include apprehending drug dealers (B), diabetes testing and diagnosis (C), or banning sales of certain foods and drinks (D).

102. B: Many older homes have lead water pipes. Running hot water can dissolve lead into the water, resulting in unacceptable levels of this toxic heavy metal in drinking water. Therefore, parents should prepare baby formula using only cold water. House dust IS considered a health risk (A); dust mites can trigger allergy symptoms including asthma, and these can be serious. Indoor CO gas often occurs, but is NOT normal OR harmless (C): CO poisoning indoors can kill pets and sicken or kill humans. While infants and young children (and adults) do need some sunlight, sun exposure IS a risk (D): babies should be kept out of direct sunlight, and young children should be protected with sunscreen and sun-protective clothing, because unprotected sun exposure causes skin damage and can lead to skin cancer.

103. C: The aorta is the human body's largest artery and originates at the heart (D), which is NOT an artery at all, but an internal organ and a muscle. The superior vena cava (A) is the second largest vein in the human body and empties into the right atrium of the heart. The pulmonary artery (B) carries de-oxygenated venous blood from the heart's right ventricle to the lungs.

104. D: The cerebellum is located in the hindbrain and regulates motor movement coordination, equilibrium/balance, and muscle tone. The medulla (A) oblongata, also located in the hindbrain, regulates breathing, heartbeat, circulation, swallowing, digestion, and other autonomic (involuntary) body functions. The midbrain (B) regulates the visual system and eye movements,

and the auditory system, and participates in controlling body movements. The cerebrum (C) regulates higher brain functions like thinking and voluntary actions.

105. C: The trigeminal nerve, which is the fifth (V) cranial nerve, controls facial sensation as well as the corneal reflex of the eye and the chewing function. The facial (seventh/VII) nerve (A) controls facial muscle movements and the front two-thirds of the tongue's taste sensation. The vagus (tenth/X) nerve (B) controls the gag reflex, and soft palate and vocal cord movements. The hypoglossal (twelfth/XII) nerve (D) controls the movements of the tongue.

106. B: The majority of digestion and absorption of the food we eat is performed by the small intestine. After the teeth and tongue break down foods physically and saliva contributes digestive enzymes to begin chemical breakdown, the stomach (A) secretes gastric fluid dissolving food into chyme, a semi-liquid substance which is then mostly digested and absorbed in the small intestine. The large intestine (C) finishes the work of digesting and absorbing food. It includes the cecum; ascending, transverse, descending, and sigmoid colons; rectum; and anus. The descending colon (D), between the transverse and sigmoid colons, stores waste for emptying into the rectum, and primarily absorbs water from waste.

107. D: Children's motor skills normally develop the fastest between the ages of two and six years. From birth to four years (A), infants lift their heads and control their eye muscles; then learn to roll over and grasp; then sit up and crawl; stand and creep by one year; learn to walk, then run, kick, jump; and by three to four years can jump up and down and stand on one leg. By five years (B), they typically can skip, broad-jump, and dress themselves. By six to seven years (C), they are skillful with throwing, catching, dodging, and directing balls, and can tie their shoelaces and color pictures.

108. A: A child with Attention Deficit Hyperactivity Disorder (ADHD) who becomes exhausted from engaging in excessive physical activity is an example of an emotional (and behavioral) condition that can affect levels of physical activity and fitness. A child with depression who avoids physical activity is also an example of this. The need to monitor a child with asthma for breathing problems during exercise (B) is an example of how a physical factor can affect physical activity and fitness levels, as are the need to monitor the exercise of a child with diabetes and coordinate it with the child's diet (C), and a physically disabled child's need for adaptive equipment (and/or alternative instructional methods) to participate in physical activities (D).

109. C: The NASPE has developed six national standards for physical education. While certainly it is good for children as well as adults to consider their diets in conjunction with physical activity for physical fitness, the NASPE's standards are focused specifically on physical *education* and hence do not address diet. The criteria included in these standards *do* directly mention health (A): the third of six standards is that a physically educated individual reaches and sustains a physical fitness level that enhances his or her health. They also *do* mention self-respect as well as social interaction as benefits (B): the fifth standard states that a physically educated individual shows behaviors reflecting self-respect and respect for others within the contexts of physical activity. These standards also *do* mention pleasure (D): the sixth standard is that the physically educated person values the benefits of physical activities, which include pleasure as well as improving and maintaining health; offering physical, personal, and social challenges; and opportunities to express oneself and interact socially with others.

110. B: The WHO's recommendations are that young people engage in at least one hour per day of aerobic activity, which strengthens the heart, lungs, and large muscle groups. This makes the

cardiovascular and respiratory systems more efficient in the absorption and transportation of oxygen. These recommendations also include at least three sessions a week of weight-bearing activity, which strengthens the bones.

Creative and Performing Arts

111. C: When EC teachers plan art activities, they should design or select projects that help young children to develop their understanding of symbolic representation (which they understand in the contexts of acquiring language, early literacy and numeracy, and pretend/make-believe play) of concepts through artworks. They should also choose activities that help develop young children's fine motor skills further, rather than waiting for them to perfect these (A). They should give children activities that engage them in exploring both the materials and the processes of art together, not sequentially (B). And teachers should also give children activities that include both the processes and products of art (D); e.g., painting pictures of animals, wherein exploring paint use is process and representing animals is product.

112. D: If all other content areas have been related to the theme of space travel, the most appropriate thing the teacher can do of the choices given for an art activity is to engage the children in constructing model rocket ships, which also relates to the established theme. Painting self-portraits (A) does not relate to this theme; it would fit better in a unit on early social studies concepts like identity and self-awareness, and/or an art unit on famous artists' self-portraits. Providing different materials and textures in the same color (B) relates to the theme of that color, not space travel. A class discussion (C) relates to the identified theme, but does not include any art activity.

113. C: A good first step in the EC art activity lesson plan is to engage the children in a preliminary discussion about the activity (A), so they understand its purpose, nature, and some of its procedures; can ask questions and contribute their ideas and experiences; and feel more prepared for the activity. A good second step is for the teacher and students to share or read books about the art activity (D), which gives them more information about it; represents some primarily nonverbal procedures in verbal description; and integrates art with literacy. Then the teacher can provide photos, reproductions, and actual artworks related to the planned activity (B), giving the children concrete examples for modeling and visual demonstrations of what they have verbally discussed and read. The last step they should take is for the teacher to dispense the needed materials and instruments (C), having the children help to assemble these in preparation for executing the hands-on activity/project.

114. B: Meret Oppenheim, an artist of the Dada movement, created a (1936) work with a teacup, saucer, and spoon all covered with hair. This work has an artistic function as it can be viewed, makes a statement, and evokes various reactions in its viewers, and a social function in the artist's protest of the war and other social issues, but no physical function as it cannot be used for any physical purpose. The raku pottery (A) has both an artistic function in its elegance and a physical function in its use of holding and drinking tea during the traditional Japanese tea ceremony. The tribal war club (C) serves an artistic function in its exquisite craftsmanship and a physical function in its use to bludgeon enemies. Therefore (D) is incorrect, as not all of these have physical functions.

115. A: Developing a personal idea of what a work of art is intended to accomplish and/or communicate represents the interpretation step of the performance process. The analysis (B) step

precedes interpretation and involves researching the artwork's background and examining its structure to comprehend the work and its meaning. The selection (C) step is the first, and involves the performer's choosing which particular work of art to perform. The evaluation (D) step follows the interpretation step. As the performer rehearses his/her application of the work to a performance, s/he evaluates this and refines that application until it is ready for presentation (which is the final step).

116. B: This is a description of the visual art component of line. By outlining the contours of an object represented two-dimensionally in art, connected lines create shapes (A). Colors (C) are the wavelengths of light that a surface reflects. Blue paint on canvas reflects only the blue wavelengths; it absorbs all other color wavelengths so we cannot see them. Form (D) is the three-dimensional version of shape. In drawings and paintings, form gives the appearance of mass; in sculptures, form has real mass. Form can also refer to the overall structure of an artwork.

117. C: Purple is defined as a secondary color, meaning it is produced by mixing two primary colors. Primary colors cannot be produced by mixing other colors, and cannot be broken down into other colors. The primary colors are red (A), blue (B), and yellow (D). Purple is produced by mixing red and blue together.

118. D: Harmony is created by playing or singing several differently pitched notes at the same time. Chords are an example of harmony. Tempo (A) is how fast or slow the speed is of playing or singing a piece of music. Rhythm (B) is the pattern created by alternating and repeating notes with different time durations. Melody (C) is created by playing or singing single, differently pitched notes in series, not at the same time, to create a musical line or tune. (A series of harmonies or chords is called a harmonic progression or chord progression rather than a melody because it is a line of grouped notes rather than single notes.)

119. B: Directions noted on musical compositions tell performers what speed and rhythm to use in playing or singing them. *Staccato* means to play or sing a series of notes separately and sharply, and is further notated by a dot above each note; *legato* means to play or sing a series of notes in a smooth, connected manner. Directions for tempi are typically named below the title and composer's name, right above the musical notation, and within the body of the composition when the tempo changes. *Andante* means "walking" in Italian and signifies a moderate speed; *lento* means "slow" (A). *Allegro* means "happy" and denotes a quick speed; *adagio* (C) means "at ease" in Italian and indicates a slow tempo that is slower than *andante* but not as slow as *largo* (D), which means "large" and indicates expansively slow in tempo. *Presto* (D) is quite fast.

120. D: The organizing principle of unity in art means the work is cohesive; all of its elements seem to belong together, and combine into a completed whole in our perceptions. We may perceive artworks lacking unity as disorganized, fragmented, incomplete, and/or as collections of disconnected parts. The organizing principle of repetition (A) in art means the artist repeats certain elements—e.g., musical themes or motifs; certain visual lines, shapes, colors, textures, etc.; certain dance steps or step combinations; or certain dramatic actions or lines of dialogue— throughout the piece to create structure, emphasis, and change to achieve desired effects. The organizing principle of contrast (B) in art means the artist combines noticeable differences in the work's elements to create interest and excitement and avoid monotony. The organizing principle of balance (C) in art means the artist achieves visual, aural, kinetic, and/or dramatic equilibrium among the various elements used in the work. Balance also contributes to unity.